POEMS AND BALLADS

OF

GOETHE

TRANSLATED BY

W. EDMONDSTOUNE AYTOUN, D.C.L.

AND

THEODORE MARTIN

NEW YORK:

DELISSER & PROCTER,

508 BROADWAY.

1859.

PREFACE.

Several years have elapsed since a considerable portion of the following translations appeared in the columns of "Blackwood's Magazine." It was then the ambition and desire of the translators to have laid before the public, through that widely-circulated medium, such a selection from the minor poems and ballads of the great German author, as might tend to convey to an English reader something like an adequate impression of his varied genius. At that time very few of these poems had appeared in an English dress; at any rate, no attempt towards a copious version had been made Goethe was well known in England by the fame of his longer works; in particular, his "Faust" was generally read, and had been frequently translated; but, comparatively speaking, few persons were acquainted with his lesser poems, upon the composition of which he bestowed the utmost amount of care and elaboration. His accomplished biographer, Mr. Lewes, has said of these, with equal truth and felicity of expression—"They are instinct with life and beauty, against which no prejudice can stand. They give musical form to feelings the most various, and to feelings that are true. They are gay, coquettish, playful, tender, passionate, mournful, reflective, and picturesque; now simple as the 'tune which beats time to nothing in your head,' now laden with weighty thought; at one moment reflecting with ethereal grace the whim and fancy of caprice, at another sobbing forth the sorrows which press a cry from the heart." Mr. Lewes is here alluding rather to the lyrics than the ballads, of which latter some may be ranked as among the most perfect and powerful of modern poetical compositions.

After having proceeded some way with their task, the translators were prevented by other avocations from completing it. It was, however, never lost sight of as a work to be carried through, should circumstances permit. Under the deep conviction that these masterpieces of literary skill ought to be approached with no reckless hand, the translators have in the interval endeavoured to overcome the difficulties of their self imposed task, and they have spared no pains to make their transcripts faithful in form as well as spirit to the originals.

They believe that the system of co-operation which they have pursued has been attended with advantage. Each translator has selected the poems to which he thought he could best do justice, and in this way he has worked with a freshness of impulse which otherwise could not have been obtained. In many cases the poems have undergone the careful revision of both the translators, and each has honestly given and accepted the criticism and correction of the other. The initial of each translator attached to the poems indicates those which are either wholly or substantially his separate work. In some instances, however, the translations are, in the strictest sense, joint productions, and to these the joint initials have been appended. The translators may perhaps be allowed to add, that they have already had some experience of the advantages of literary co-operation; for a volume of humorous poems and *jeux d'esprit* issued by them, several years ago, under the title of "Bon Gaultier's Ballads," has been fortunate enough to obtain a wide circulation.

The translators need hardly say that they have not attempted a version of all, or even of the majority of Goethe's minor poems. The vast number of these would, of itself, have been sufficient to deter them from any such attempt; but, besides this, many of them are really of slight intrinsic value. Every voluminous author has been unequal in his efforts. Goethe, who was the most industrious and indefatigable literary man of the age, was no exception to this rule. His wheat, though of the finest quality, has not been so well winnowed that the chaff has entirely disappeared. Further, some of the minor poems are valuable solely, or nearly so, for the neatness of their workmanship, and the charm of these is not to be transferred to another language. Others are either of exclusively biographical interest, or cast in forms alien to the genius of the English language. The former do not fall within the scope of a work like the present; the latter would have been so much altered by the process of recasting, as to assume the appearance of original rather than of translated poems. The admirable series of compositions in hexameter and pentameter verse, including "The Roman Elegies," "Alexis and Dora," and others, which in themselves are among the most finished of Goethe's poetical works, the translators do not believe can be rendered, by any amount of labour and skill, into corresponding English measures with any assurance of success. At the same time, it was with no small reluctance that they abandoned the classical measures in the case of the series of poems "In the Manner of the Antique." But believing the idea of these exquisite pieces to be more important than the form, and to be separable from the form without serious detriment, they decided on adopting the metres which in their opinion would best commend them to the taste of English readers. For, after all, it is for them, and not for German scholars, that this volume has been written. Wherever, as in the case of the poems in irregular unrhymed metres, it seemed possible to preserve the form without injury, and indeed with advantage to the enjoyment of the poem, the translators have endeavoured to illustrate the rhythmical capabilities of our English speech, which they believe to be far greater than is generally supposed. Unwilling, however, to press this experiment too far, they have left unattempted several poems of this class, which they might otherwise have included in their volume.

In conclusion, the translators may observe that they cannot hope altogether to escape that censure which follows every attempt at selection. Some critics may think that they have included a few poems which might have been advantageously omitted; others that they have been too fastidious in their exclusions. Perhaps they may have erred in both ways. But they can say, in all honesty, that they have executed their work according to the best of their judgment and ability; and, with that declaration, they humbly take their leave.

CONTENTS.

BALLADS AND LEGENDS.

MISCELLANEOUS POEMS.

SONGS AND LYRICS.

NOTES.

POEMS AND BALLADS OF GOETHE.

GOETHE'S INTRODUCTION.

This somewhat mystical and rather unsatisfactory composition, which appears by way of preface to the author's miscellaneous poems, is certainly not conceived in his happiest manner, though, like all his other writings, it has been most carefully elaborated. It seems intended to supply the place of the invocation to the muse, with which the ancient poets almost invariably commenced as a sort of sanctifying ceremony; but the custom, appropriate enough so long as the inspiration of the sacred Nine was acknowledged, or even typically accepted, has now fallen into general disuse. The substitution of the Goddess of Nature, or the Genius of Poetry, appears to our English taste but a clumsy expedient. Goethe, however, thought otherwise; and his example has since been followed by various German poets of lesser note, who have vouchsafed to us glimpses of their communings with some visionary Egeria.

I.

THE morning came. Its footsteps scared away
The gentle sleep that hover'd lightly o'er me;
I left my quiet cot to greet the day,
And gaily climb'd the mountain-side before me.

The sweet young flowers! how fresh were they and
tender,
Brimful with dew upon the sparkling lea;
The young day open'd in exulting splendour,
And all around seem'd glad to gladden me.

II.

And, as I mounted, o'er the meadow ground
A white and filmy essence 'gan to hover;
It sail'd and shifted till it hemm'd me round,
Then rose above my head, and floated over.
No more I saw the beauteous scene unfolded—
It lay beneath a melancholy shroud;
And soon was I, as if in vapour moulded,
Alone, within the twilight of the cloud.

III.

At once, as though the sun were struggling through,
Within the mist a sudden radiance started;
Here sunk the vapour, but to rise anew,
There on the peak, and upland forest parted.
O, how I panted for the first clear gleaming,
Made by the gloom it banish'd doubly bright!
It came not, but a glory round me beaming,
And I stood blinded by the gush of light.

IV.

A moment, and I felt enforc'd to look,
By some strange impulse of the heart's emotion;
But more than one quick glance I scarce could brook,
For all was burning like a molten ocean.
There, in the glorious clouds that seem'd to bear her,
A form angelic hover'd in the air;
Ne'er did my eyes behold a vision fairer,
And still she gazed upon me, floating there.

V.

"Dost thou not know me?" and her voice was soft
As truthful love, and holy calm it sounded.
"Know'st thou not me, who many a time and oft
Poured balsam in thy hurts when sorest wounded?
Ah, well thou knowest her, to whom for ever
Thy heart in union pants to be allied!
Have I not seen the tears—the wild endeavour
That even in boyhood brought thee to my side?"

VI.

"Yes! I have felt thy influence oft," I cried,
And sank on earth before her, half-adoring;
"Thou brought'st me rest when Passion's lava tide
Thro' my young veins like liquid fire was pouring.

And thou hast fann'd, as with celestial pinions,
In summer's heat, my parch'd and fever'd brow;
Gav'st me the choicest gifts of earth's dominions,
And, save through thee, I seek no fortune now.

VII.

"I name thee not, but I have heard thee nam'd,
And heard thee styled their own ere now by many;
All eyes believe at thee their glance is aim'd,
Though thine effulgence is too great for any.
Ah! I had many comrades whilst I wander'd—
I know thee now, and stand almost alone:
I veil thy light, too precious to be squander'd,
And share the inward joy I feel with none."

VIII.

Smiling, she said—"Thou seest 'twas wise from thee
To keep the fuller, greater revelation:
Scarce art thou from grotesque delusions free,
Scarce master of thy childish first sensation;
Yet deem'st thyself so far above thy brothers,
That thou hast won the right to scorn them! Cease.

Who made the yawning gulf 'twixt thee and others?
  Know—know thyself—live with the world in
    peace."

IX.

"Forgive me!" I exclaim'd, "I meant no ill,
  Else should in vain my eyes be disenchanted;
Within my blood there stirs a genial will—
  I know the worth of all that thou hast granted.
That boon I hold in trust for others merely,
  Nor shall I let it rust within the ground;
Why sought I out the pathway so sincerely,
  If not to guide my brothers to the bound?"

X.

And as I spoke, upon her radiant face
  Pass'd a sweet smile, like breath across a mirror;
And in her eyes' bright meaning I could trace
  What I had answer'd well, and what in error.
She smiled, and then my heart regain'd its lightness,
  And bounded in my breast with rapture high:
Then durst I pass within her zone of brightness,
  And gaze upon her with unquailing eye.

XI.

Straightway she stretch'd her hand among the thin
And watery haze that round her presence hover'd;
Slowly it coil'd and shrunk her grasp within,
And lo! the landscape lay once more uncover'd—
Again mine eye could scan the sparkling meadow,
I look'd to heaven, and all was clear and bright;
I saw her hold a veil without a shadow,
That undulated round her in the light.

XII.

"I know thee!—all thy weakness, all that yet
Of good within thee lives and glows, I've measur'd;"
She said—her voice I never may forget—
"Accept the gift that long for thee was treasur'd.
Oh! happy he, thrice-bless'd in earth and heaven,
Who takes this gift with soul serene and true,
The veil of song, by Truth's own fingers given,
Enwoven of sunshine and the morning dew.

XIII.

"Wave but this veil on high, whene'er beneath
The noonday fervour thou and thine are glowing,

And fragrance of all flowers around shall breathe,
And the cool winds of eve come freshly blowing.
Earth's cares shall cease for thee, and all its riot;
Where gloom'd the grave, a starry couch be seen;
The waves of life shall sink in halcyon quiet;
The days be lovely fair, the nights serene."

XIV.

Come then, my friends, and whether 'neath the load
Of heavy griefs ye struggle on, or whether
Your better destiny shall strew the road
With flowers, and golden fruits that cannot wither,
United let us move, still forward striving;
So while we live shall joy our days illume,
And in our children's hearts our love surviving
Shall gladden them, when we are in the tomb.

A. M.

POEMS

IN THE MANNER OF THE ANTIQUE.

THE short poems, of which the following are translations, were composed by Goethe at different periods, and finally collected and arranged under the above title. They bear a strong resemblance to the better portion of the Greek Anthology, so far as regards the compression and delicate nature of the thoughts, and also the extreme felicity of the language. In the original German they are cast in the ancient hexameter and pentameter, which no doubt enhances the resemblance, and which the translators would have adopted, but from a sincere conviction that these metres are unsuited to the genius of the English speech. Upon this subject there has been a good deal of controversy, from the days of Southey downwards; and many ingenious attempts have been made to prove that it is possible, by care and dexterity, to construct a good English poem in the classical form. Without denying the possibility (which it would be hazardous to do in the face of such an example as Mr. Longfellow's "Evangeline"), the translators nevertheless maintain their opinion that such versification is entirely exotic, and not calculated either to make the same impression or to give the same pleasure as a skilful use of the standard English metres, of which there is a sufficient variety for every phonetic purpose. They have, therefore, in the rendering of this section of Goethe's poetry, departed from their general rule of adhering as closely as may be to the form of the originals; and they venture to think that, by doing so, they have made a nearer approximation to the spirit of these really beautiful poems than could be effected by the adoption of the ancient metrical system.

THE CHOSEN ROCK.

Here, in the hush and stillness of mid-noon,
The lover lay, and thought upon his love;
With blithesome voice he spoke to me: "Be thou
My witness, stone!—Yet, therefore, vaunt thee not,
For thou hast many partners of my joy—
To every rock that crowns this grassy dell,
And looks on me and my felicity;
To every forest-stem that I embrace
In my entrancement as I roam along,
Stand thou for a memorial of my bliss!
All mingle with my rapture, and to all
I lift a consecrating cry of joy.
Yet do I lend a voice to thee alone,
As culls the Muse some favourite from the crowd,
And, with a kiss, inspires for evermore."

M.

ANACREON'S GRAVE.

Where the rose is fresh and blooming—where the vine and myrtle spring—
Where the turtle-dove is cooing—where the gay cicalas sing—
Whose may be the grave surrounded with such store of comely grace,
Like a God-created garden? 'Tis Anacreon's resting-place.
Spring and summer and the autumn pour'd their gifts around the bard,
And, ere winter came to chill him, sound he slept beneath the sward.

A.

THE CHINAMAN IN ROME.

In Rome I saw a stranger from Pekin:
Uncouth and heavy to his eye appear'd
The mingled piles of old and modern time.
"Alas!" he said, "what wretched taste is here!
When will they learn to stretch the airy roof
On light pilaster'd shafts of varnish'd wood—

Gain the fine sense, and educated eye,
Which only finds in lacquer, carvings quaint,
And variegated tintings, pure delight?"
Hearing these words, unto myself I said,
"Behold the type of many a moon-struck bard,
Who vaunts his tissue, woven of a dream,
'Gainst Nature's tapestry, that lasts for aye,
Proclaims as sick the truly sound; and this,
That he, the truly sick, may pass for sound!"

M.

THE PARK.

How beautiful! A garden fair as heaven,
Flowers of all hues, and smiling in the sun,
Where all was waste and wilderness before.
Well do ye imitate, ye gods of earth,
The great Creator. Rock, and lake, and glade,
Birds, fishes, and untamèd beasts are here.
Your work were all an Eden, but for this—
Here is no man unconscious of a pang,
No perfect Sabbath of unbroken rest.

M.

PERFECT BLISS.

All the divine perfections, which, whilere
Nature in thrift doled out 'mongst many a fair,
She shower'd with open hand, thou peerless one, on thee!
And she that was so wondrously endow'd,
To whom a throng of noble knees were bow'd,
Gave all—Love's perfect gift—her glorious self, to me!

M.

SOLITUDE.

Grant, O ye healing Nymphs, that have your haunts
By rock and stream and lonely forest-glade,
The boon which, in their bosoms' silent depths,
Your votaries crave! Unto the sad of heart
Give comfort—knowledge unto him that doubts—
Possession to the lover, and its joy.
For unto you the Gods have given, what they
Denied to man—to aid and to console
All those soe'er, who put their trust in you.

M.

PHILOMELA.

Surely, surely, Amor nursed thee, songstress of the plaintive note,
And, in fond and childish fancy, fed thee from his pointed dart.
So, sweet Philomel, the poison sunk into thy guileless throat,
Till, with all love's weight of passion, strike its notes to every heart.

M.

THE HUSBANDMAN.

Lightly doth the furrow fold the golden grain within its breast,
Deeper shroud, old man, shall cover in thy limbs when laid at rest.
Blithely plough, and sow as blithely! Here are springs of mortal cheer,
And when e'en the grave is closing, Hope is ever standing near.

M.

WARNING.

Do not touch him—do not wake him! Fast asleep is Amor lying;
Go—fulfil thy work appointed—do thy labour of the day.
Thus the wise and careful mother uses every moment flying,
Whilst her child is in the cradle—Slumbers pass too soon away.

A.

THE BROTHERS.

Slumber, Sleep—they were two brothers, servants to the Gods above;
Kind Prometheus lur'd them downwards, ever fill'd with earthly love;
But what Gods could bear so lightly, press'd too hard on men beneath;
Slumber did his brother's duty—Sleep was deepen'd into Death.

A.

LOVE'S HOUR-GLASS.

Eros! wherefore do I see thee, with the glass in either hand?
Fickle God! with double measure wouldst thou count the shifting sand?
"*This* one flows for parted lovers—slowly drops each tiny bead—
That is for the days of dalliance, and it melts with golden speed."

A.

THE TEACHERS.

What time Diogenes, unmoved and still,
Lay in his tub, and bask'd him in the sun—
What time Calanus clomb, with lightsome step
And smiling cheek, up to his fiery tomb—
What rare examples there for Philip's son
To curb his overmastering lust of sway,
But that the Lord of the majestic world
Was all too great for lessons even like these!

M.

THE WREATHS.

Our German Klopstock, if he had his will,
Would bar us from the skirts of Pindus old.
No more the classic laurel should be priz'd,
But the rough leaflets of our native oak
Alone should glisten in the poet's hair;
Yet did himself, with spirit unreclaim'd
From first allegiance to those early Gods,
Lead up to Golgotha's most awful height
With more than epic pomp the new Crusade.
But let him range the bright angelic host
On either hill—no matter. By his grave
All gentle hearts should bow them down and weep.
For where a hero and a saint have died,
Or where a poet sang prophetical,
Dying as greatly as they greatly lived,
To give memorial to all after-times,
Of lofty worth and courage undismay'd;
There, in mute reverence, all devoutly kneel,
In homage of the thorn and laurel wreath,
That were at once their glory and their pang!

A.

SACRED GROUND.

A PLACE to mark the Graces, when they come
Down from Olympus, still and secretly,
To join the Oreads in their festival,
Beneath the light of the benignant moon.
There lies the poet, watching them unseen,
The whilst they chant the sweetest songs of heaven,
Or, floating o'er the sward without a sound,
Lead on the mystic wonder of the dance.
All that is great in heaven, or fair on earth,
Unveils its glories to the dreamer's eye,
And all he tells the Muses. They again,
Knowing that Gods are jealous of their own,
Teach him, through all the passion of his verse,
To utter these high secrets reverently.

A.

THE MUSE'S MIRROR.

To deck herself, the Muse, at early morn,
Wander'd adown a wimpling brook, to find
Some glassy pool more quiet than the rest.

On sped the stream, and ever as it ran
It swept away her image, which did change
With every bend and dimple of the wave.
In wrath the Goddess turn'd her from the spot,
Yet after her the brook, with taunting tongue,
Did call—"'Tis plain thou wilt not see the truth,
All purely though my mirror shows it thee!"
But she, meanwhile, stood with indifferent ear,
By a far corner of the crystal lake,
Delightedly surveying her fair form,
And settling flowerets in her golden hair.

M.

EXCULPATION.

Wilt thou dare to blame the woman for her seeming sudden changes,
Swaying east and swaying westward, as the breezes shake the tree?
Fool! thy selfish thought misguides thee—find the *man* that never ranges;
Woman wavers but to seek him—Is not then the fault in thee?

A.

THE SWISS ALP.

Yesterday thy head was brown, as are the flowing
locks of love,
In the bright blue sky I watch'd thee towering, giant-
like, above.
Now thy summit, white and hoary, glitters all with
silver snow,
Which the stormy night hath shaken from its robes
upon thy brow;
And I know that youth and age are bound with such
mysterious meaning,
As the days are link'd together, one short dream but
intervening.

A.

MARRIAGE UNEQUAL.

Alas, that even in a heavenly marriage,
The fairest lots should ne'er be reconcil'd!
Psyche wax'd old, and prudent in her carriage,
Whilst Cupid evermore remains the child.

A.

THE NEW LOVE.

Love, not the simple youth that whilom wound
Himself about young Psyche's heart, looked round
Olympus with a cold and roving eye,
That had accustom'd been to victory.
It rested on a Goddess, noblest far
Of all that noble throng—a glorious star—
Venus Urania. And from that hour
He loved her. Ah! to his resistless power
Even she, the holy one, did yield at last,
And in his daring arms he held her fast.
A new and beauteous Love from that embrace
Had birth, which to the mother owed his grace
And purity of soul, whilst from his sire
He borrow'd all his passion, all his fire.
Him ever, where the gracious Muses be,
Thou'lt surely find. Such sweet society
Is his delight, and his sharp-pointed dart
Doth rouse within men's breasts the love of Art.

M.

PHŒBUS AND HERMES.

THE deep-brow'd lord of Delos once, and Maia's nimble-witted son,
Contended eagerly by whom the prize of glory should be won;
Hermes long'd to grasp the lyre,—the lyre Apollo hoped to gain,
And both their hearts were full of hope, and yet the hopes of both were vain.
For Ares, to decide the strife, between them rudely dash'd in ire,
And waving high his falchion keen, he cleft in twain the golden lyre.
Loud Hermes laugh'd maliciously, but at the direful deed did fall
The deepest grief upon the heart of Phœbus and the Muses all.

M.

HOLY FAMILY.

O child of beauty rare—
O mother chaste and fair—
How happy seem they both, so far beyond compar !
She, in her infant blest,
And he in conscious rest,
Nestling within the soft warm cradle of her breast!
What joy that sight might bear
To him who sees them there,
If, with a pure and guilt-untroubled eye,
He look'd upon the twain, like Joseph standing by.

A.

BALLADS AND LEGENDS.

THE BRIDE OF CORINTH.

Of this poem, which is acknowledged to be a masterpiece, Mrs. Austin has said very happily, "An awful and undefined horror breathes throughout it. In the slow measured rhythm of the verse, and the pathetic simplicity of the diction, there is a solemnity and a stirring spell which chains the feelings like a deep mysterious strain of music." Several attempts have been made to translate it into English, but in no previous instance has the exact metre of the original been adhered to, owing, no doubt, to the poverty of our language in double rhymes. It is hardly necessary to observe that all great composers have taken especial care to adopt, vary, or modify their metres according to the peculiar tone and character of the poem; and, in this instance, it appeared to the translators, that by no other form of verse except that which Goethe had selected could this poem be rendered so as to convey to the English reader a due impression of its power. Therefore they resolved, whatever amount of labour the effort might require, to overcome the metrical difficulty; and so much at least they have been able, by mutual co-operation, to accomplish. Their success, however, they are well aware, must be estimated according to their fidelity to the original, the expression of which they have striven throughout to maintain without any kind of alteration.

I.

A youth to Corinth, whilst the city slumber'd,
Came from Athens: though a stranger there,
Soon among its townsmen to be number'd,
For a bride awaits him, young and fair:
From their childhood's years
They were plighted feres,
So contracted by their parents' care.

II.

But may not his welcome there be hinder'd?
Dearly must he buy it, would he speed.
He is still a heathen with his kindred,
She and hers wash'd in the Christian creed.
When new faiths are born,
Love and troth are torn
Rudely from the heart, howe'er it bleed.

III.

All the house is hush'd;—to rest retreated
Father, daughters—not the mother quite;
She the guest with cordial welcome greeted,
Led him to a room with tapers bright;

Wine and food she brought,
Ere of them he thought,
Then departed with a fair good-night.

IV.

But he felt no hunger, and unheeded
Left the wine, and eager for the rest
Which his limbs, forspent with travel, needed,
On the couch he laid him, still undress'd.
There he sleeps—when lo!
Onwards gliding slow,
At the door appears a wondrous guest.

V.

By the waning lamp's uncertain gleaming
There he sees a youthful maiden stand,
Robed in white, of still and gentle seeming,
On her brow a black and golden band.
When she meets his eyes,
With a quick surprise
Starting, she uplifts a pallid hand.

VI.

"Is a stranger here, and nothing told me?
Am I then forgotten even in name?

Ah! 'tis thus within my cell they hold me,
And I now am cover'd o'er with shame!
Pillow still thy head
There upon thy bed,
I will leave thee quickly as I came."

VII.

"Maiden—darling! Stay, O stay!" and, leaping
From the couch, before her stands the boy:
"Ceres—Bacchus, here their gifts are heaping,
And thou bringest Amor's gentle joy!
Why with terror pale?
Sweet one, let us hail
These bright gods—their festive gifts employ."

VIII.

"Oh, no—no! Young stranger, come not nigh me;
Joy is not for me, nor festive cheer.
Ah! such bliss may ne'er be tasted by me,
Since my mother, in fantastic fear,
By long sickness bow'd,
To Heaven's service vow'd
Me, and all the hopes that warm'd me here.

IX.

"They have left our hearth, and left it lonely—
The old gods, that bright and jocund train.
One, unseen, in heaven, is worshipp'd only,
And upon the cross a Saviour slain;
Sacrifice is here,
Not of lamb nor steer,
But of human woe and human pain."

X.

And he asks, and all her words doth ponder—
"Can it be, that, in this silent spot,
I behold thee, thou surpassing wonder!
My sweet bride, so strangely to me brought?
Be mine only now—
See, our parents' vow
Heaven's good blessing hath for us besought."

XI.

"No! thou gentle heart," she cried in anguish;
"'Tis not mine, but 'tis my sister's place;
When in lonely cell I weep and languish,
Think, oh think of me in her embrace!

I think but of thee—
Pining drearily,
Soon beneath the earth to hide my face!"

XII.

"Nay! I swear by yonder flame which burneth,
Fann'd by Hymen, lost thou shalt not be;
Droop not thus, for my sweet bride returneth
To my father's mansion back with me!
Dearest! tarry here!
Taste the bridal cheer,
For our spousal spread so wondrously!"

XIII.

Then with word and sign their troth they plighted,
Golden was the chain she bade him wear;
But the cup he offer'd her she slighted,
Silver, wrought with cunning past compare.
"That is not for me;
All I ask of thee
Is one little ringlet of thy hair."

XIV.

Dully boom'd the midnight hour unhallow'd,
And then first her eyes began to shine;

Eagerly with pallid lips she swallow'd
Hasty draughts of purple-tinctured wine;
But the wheaten bread,
As in shuddering dread,
Put she always by with loathing sign.

XV.

And she gave the youth the cup: he drain'd it,
With impetuous haste he drain'd it dry;
Love was in his fever'd heart, and pain'd it,
Till it ached for joys she must deny.
But the maiden's fears
Stay'd him, till in tears
On the bed he sank, with sobbing cry.

XVI.

And she leans above him—"Dear one, still thee!
Ah, how sad am I to see thee so!
But, alas! these limbs of mine would chill thee:
Love! they mantle not with passion's glow;
Thou wouldst be afraid,
Didst thou find the maid
Thou hast chosen, cold as ice or snow."

XVII.

Round her waist his eager arms he bended,
  With the strength that youth and love inspire;
"Wert thou even from the grave ascended,
  I could warm thee well with my desire!"
      Panting kiss on kiss!
      Overflow of bliss!
  "Burn'st thou not, and feelest me on fire?"

XVIII.

Closer yet they cling, and intermingling,
  Tears and broken sobs proclaim the rest;
His hot breath through all her frame is tingling,
  There they lie, caressing and caress'd.
      His impassion'd mood
      Warms her torpid blood,
  Yet there beats no heart within her breast!

XIX.

Meanwhile goes the mother, softly creeping,
  Through the house, on needful cares intent,
Hears a murmur, and, while all are sleeping,
  Wonders at the sounds, and what they meant.

Who was whispering so?—
Voices soft and low,
In mysterious converse strangely blent.

XX.

Straightway by the door herself she stations,
There to be assur'd what was amiss;
And she hears love's fiery protestations,
Words of ardour and endearing bliss:
"Hark, the cock! 'Tis light!
But to-morrow night
Thou wilt come again?"—and kiss on kiss.

XXI.

Quick the latch she raises, and, with features
Anger-flush'd, into the chamber hies.
"Are there in my house such shameless creatures,
Minions to the stranger's will?" she cries.
By the dying light,
Who is't meets her sight?
God! 'tis her own daughter she espies!

XXII.

And the youth in terror sought to cover,
With her own light veil, the maiden's head,

Clasp'd her close; but, gliding from her lover,
  Back the vestment from her brow she spread,
      And her form upright,
      As with ghostly might,
  Long and slowly rises from the bed.

XXIII.

"Mother! mother! wherefore thus deprive me
  Of such joy as I this night have known?
Wherefore from these warm embraces drive me?
  Was I waken'd up to meet thy frown?
      Did it not suffice
      That, in virgin guise,
  To an early grave you brought me down?

XXIV.

"Fearful is the weird that forc'd me hither,
  From the dark-heap'd chamber where I lay;
Powerless are your drowsy anthems, neither
  Can your priests prevail, howe'er they pray.
      Salt nor lymph can cool,
      Where the pulse is full;
  Love must still burn on, though wrapp'd in clay.

XXV.

"To this youth my early troth was plighted,
  Whilst yet Venus ruled within the land;
Mother! and that vow ye falsely slighted,
  At your new and gloomy faith's command.
      But no god will hear,
      If a mother swear
  Pure from love to keep her daughter's hand.

XXVI.

"Nightly from my narrow chamber driven,
  Come I to fulfil my destin'd part,
Him to seek to whom my troth was given,
  And to draw the life-blood from his heart.
      He hath served my will;
      More I yet must kill,
  For another prey I now depart.

XXVII.

"Fair young man! thy thread of life is broken,
  Human skill can bring no aid to thee.
There thou hast my chain—a ghastly token—
  And this lock of thine I take with me.

Soon must thou decay,
Soon wilt thou be grey,
Dark although to-night thy tresses be!

XXVIII.

"Mother! hear, oh hear my last entreaty!
Let the funeral-pile arise once more;
Open up my wretched tomb for pity,
And in flames our souls to peace restore.
When the ashes glow,
When the fire-sparks flow,
To the ancient gods aloft we soar."

A. M.

THE ERL-KING.

Who rides so late through the grisly night?
'Tis a father and child, and he grasps him tight;
He wraps him close in his mantle's fold,
And shelters the boy from the piercing cold.

"My son, why thus to my arm dost cling?"
"Father, dost thou not see the Erlie-king?
The king with his crown and his long black train!"
"My son, 'tis a streak of the misty rain!"

"Come hither, thou darling! come, go with me!
Fine games know I that I'll play with thee;
Flowers many and bright do my kingdoms hold,
My mother has many a robe of gold.

"Oh father, dear father! and dost thou not hear
What the Erlie-king whispers so low in mine ear?"
"Calm, calm thee, my boy, it is only the breeze,
As it rustles the wither'd leaves under the trees!"

"Wilt thou go, bonny boy! wilt thou go with me?
My daughters shall wait on thee daintilie;
My daughters around thee in dance shall sweep,
And rock thee, and kiss thee, and sing thee to sleep!"

"O father, dear father! and dost thou not mark
Erlie-king's daughters move by in the dark?"
"I see it, my child; but it is not they,
'Tis the old willow nodding its head so grey!"

"I love thee! thy beauty, it charms me so;
And I'll take thee by force, if thou wilt not go!"
"O father, dear father! he's grasping me—
My heart is as cold as cold can be!"

The father rides swiftly—with terror he gasps—
The sobbing child in his arms he clasps;
He reaches the castle with spurring and dread;
But, alack! in his arms the child lay dead!

M.

THE FISHER.

The water rush'd and bubbled by—
  An angler near it lay,
And watch'd his quill, with tranquil eye,
  Upon the current play.
And as he sits in wasteful dream,
  He sees the flood unclose,
And from the middle of the stream
  A river-maiden rose.

She sang to him with witching wile,
  "My brood why wilt thou snare,
With human craft and human guile,
  To die in scorching air?
Ah! didst thou know how happy we,
  Who dwell in waters clear,
Thou wouldst come down at once to me,
  And rest for ever here.

"The sun and ladye-moon they lave
  Their tresses in the main,
And, breathing freshness from the wave,
  Come doubly bright again.
The deep-blue sky, so moist and clear,
  Hath it for thee no lure?
Does thine own face not woo thee down
  Unto our waters pure?"

The water rush'd and bubbled by—
  It lapp'd his naked feet;
He thrill'd as though he felt the touch
  Of maiden kisses sweet.
She spoke to him, she sang to him—
  Resistless was her strain—
Half-drawn, he sank beneath the wave,
  And ne'er was seen again.

M.

THE GOD AND THE BAYADERÉ.

AN INDIAN LEGEND.

I.

MAHADEH, earth's lord, descending,
To its mansions comes again,
That, like man with mortals blending,
He may feel their joy and pain;
Stoops to try life's varied changes,
And with human eyes to see,
Ere he praises or avenges,
What their fitful lot may be.
He has pass'd thro' the city, has look'd on them all;
He has watch'd o'er the great, nor forgotten the small,
And at evening went forth on his journey so free.

II.

In the outskirts of the city,
Where the straggling huts are piled,
At a casement stood a pretty
Painted thing, almost a child.

"Greet thee, maiden!" "Thanks—art weary?
Wait, and quickly I'll appear!"
"What art thou?"—"A Bayaderé,
And the home of love is here."
She rises; the cymbals she strikes as she dances,
And whirling, and bending with grace, she advances,
And offers him flowers, as she undulates near.

III.

O'er the threshold gliding lightly,
In she leads him to her room.
"Fear not, gentle stranger; brightly
Shall my lamp dispel the gloom.
Art thou weary? I'll relieve thee—
Bathe thy feet, and soothe their smart;
All thou askest I can give thee—
Rest, or song, or joy impart."
She labours to soothe him, she labours to please;
The Deity smiles; for with pleasure he sees
Through deep degradation a right-loving heart.

IV.

And he asks for service menial,
And she only strives the more,

Nature's impulse now is genial,
  Where but art prevail'd before.
As the fruit succeeds the blossom,
  Swells and ripens day by day,
So, where kindness fills the bosom,
  Love is never far away.
But he, whose vast motive was deeper and higher,
Selected, more keenly and clearly to try her,
Love, follow'd by anguish, and death, and dismay.

V.

And her rosy cheeks he presses,
  And she feels love's torment sore,
And, thrill'd through by his caresses,
  Weeps, who never wept before.
Droops beside him, not dissembling,
  Or for passion or for gain,
But her limbs grow faint and trembling,
  And no more their strength retain.
Meanwhile the still hours of the night stealing by
Spread their shadowy woof o'er the face of the sky,
Bringing love and its festival joys in their train.

VI.

Light she slept, her arms around him;
  Waking soon from broken rest,
Dead upon her breast she found him,
  Dead—that dearly-cherish'd guest!
With a shriek, she flings her o'er him,
  But he answers not her cry;
And unto the pile they bore him,
  Stark of limb and cold of eye.
She hears the priests chanting—she hears the death-song,
And frantic she rises, and bursts through the throng.
"Who is she? what seeks she? why comes she so nigh?"

VII.

But the bier she falleth over,
  And her shrieks are loud and shrill—
"I *will* have my lord, my lover!
  In the grave I seek him still.
Shall that godlike frame be wasted
  By the fire's consuming blight?
Mine it was—yea mine! though tasted
  Only one delicious night!"

But the priests, they chant ever—"We carry the old,
When their watching is over, their journeys are
told;
We carry the young, when they pass from the light!

VIII.

"Hear us, woman! He we carry
Was not, could not be, thy spouse.
Art thou not a Bayaderé?
So hast thou no nuptial vows.
Only to death's silent hollow,
With the body goes the shade;
Only wives their husbands follow:
Thus alone is duty paid.
Strike loud the wild turmoil of drum and of gong!
Receive him, ye gods, in your glorious throng—
Receive him in garments of burning array'd!"

IX.

Harsh their words, and unavailing;
Swift she threaded through the quire,
And with arms outstretch'd, unquailing
Leap'd into the crackling fire.

But the deed alone sufficeth—
  Robed in might and majesty,
From the pile the god ariseth
  With the ransom'd one on high.
Divinity joys in a sinner repenting,
And the lost ones of earth, by immortals relenting,
Are wafted on pinions of fire to the sky!

A. M.

THE TREASURE-SEEKER.

I.

Many weary days I suffer'd,
  Sick of heart and poor of purse;
Riches are the greatest blessing—
  Poverty the deepest curse!
Till at last to dig a treasure
  Forth I went into the wood—
"Fiend! my soul is thine for ever!"
  And I sign'd the scroll with blood.

II.

Then I drew the magic circles,
  Kindled the mysterious fire,
Placed the herbs and bones in order,
  Spoke the incantation dire.
And I sought the buried metal
  With a spell of mickle might—
Sought it as my master taught me;
  Black and stormy was the night.

III.

And I saw a light appearing
  In the distance, like a star;
When the midnight hour was tolling,
  Came it waxing from afar:
Came it flashing, swift and sudden,
  As if fiery wine it were,
Flowing from an open chalice,
  Which a beauteous boy did bear.

IV.

And he wore a lustrous chaplet,
  And his eyes were full of thought,
As he stepp'd into the circle
  With the radiance that he brought.
And he bade me taste the goblet;
  And I thought—"It cannot be,
That this boy should be the bearer
  Of the Demon's gifts to me!"

V.

"Taste the draught of pure existence
  Sparkling in this golden urn,

And no more with baleful magic
  Shalt thou hitherward return.
Do not seek for treasures longer;
  Let thy future spellwords be,
Days of labour, nights of resting:
  So shall peace return to thee!"

A.

THE MINSTREL.

"WHAT sounds are those I hear, along
The drawbridge sweetly stealing?
Within our hall I'd have that song,
That minstrel measure, pealing."
Then forth the little foot-page hied;
When he came back, the king he cried,
"Bring in the aged minstrel!"

"Good-even to you, lordlings all;
Fair ladies all, good-even.
Lo, star on star! Within this hall
I see a radiant heaven.
In hall so bright with noble light,
'Tis not for thee to feast thy sight,
Old man, look not around thee!"

He closed his eyne, he struck his lyre
In tones with passion laden,

Till every gallant's eye shot fire,
  And down look'd every maiden.
The king, enraptured with his strain,
Held out to him a golden chain,
  In guerdon of his harping.

"The golden chain give not to me,
  For noble's breast its glance is,
Who meets and beats thy enemy,
  Amid the shock of lances.
Or give it to thy chancellere—
Let him its golden burden bear,
  Among his other burdens.

"I sing as sings the bird, whose note
  The leafy bough is heard on.
The song that falters from my throat
  For me is ample guerdon.
Yet I'd ask one thing, an I might,
A draught of brave wine, sparkling bright
  Within a golden beaker!"

The cup was brought. He drain'd its lees,
  "O draught that warms me cheerly!

Blest is the house, where gifts like these
  Are counted trifles merely.
Lo, when you prosper, think on me,
And thank your God as heartily,
  As for this draught I thank you!"

M.

THE VIOLET.

A violet blossom'd on the lea,
  Half hidden from the eye,
As fair a flower as you might see;
  When there came tripping by
A shepherd maiden fair and young,
  Lightly, lightly o'er the lea;
Care she knew not, and she sung
    Merrily!

"O were I but the fairest flower,
  That blossoms on the lea;

If only for one little hour,
  That she might gather me—
Clasp me in her bonny breast!"
  Thought the little flower.
"O that in it I might rest
    But an hour!"

Lack-a-day! Up came the lass,
  Heeded not the violet;
Trod it down into the grass;
  Though it died, 'twas happy yet.
"Trodden down although I lie,
  Yet my death is very sweet—
O the happiness to die
    At her feet!"

M.

THE

SEVEN SLEEPERS OF EPHESUS.

Six young men of Cæsar's household
Fled before their master's anger;
As a god he claim'd their worship,
Though a sorry god was he.
For an insect, ever buzzing,
Still annoy'd him at the banquet,
Still disturb'd his rest and pleasure.
All the chasing of his servants
Could not drive away the torment.
Ever round the head of Cæsar
Did the angry creature hover,
Threatening with its poison'd sting:
Still it flew, and swiftly circling
Made confusion at the table,
Messenger of Baalzebub,
The infernal Lord of flies.

"Ha!"—so spake the youths together—
"He a God that fears an insect!
Can a God be thus molested?
Does a God, like wretched mortals,
Feast and revel at the banquet?
Nay! to Him, the one, the only,
Who the sun and moon created,
Who hath made the stars in glory,
Shall we henceforth bend the knee!"

So they spake, and left the palace,
Left it in their trim apparel;
By a shepherd led, they hasten'd
To a cave was in the mountain,
And they all went gliding in.
And the shepherd's dog came after,
Though they strove to drive him from them;
Thrust himself toward his master,
Licked their hands in dumb entreaty,
That he might remain their fellow;
And lay down with them to sleep.

But the wrath of Cæsar kindled,
When he knew that they had left him;

All his former love departed,
All his thought was vengeance only.
Out in quest he sent his people,
Traced them to the mountain-hollow.
Not to fire nor sword he doom'd them;
But he bade great stones be lifted
To the entrance of the cavern;
Saw it fasten'd up with mortar;
And so left them in their tomb.

But the youths lay calmly sleeping;
And the angel, their protector,
Spake before the throne of glory:
"I have watch'd beside the sleepers,
Made them turn in slumber ever,
That the damps of yonder cavern
Should not cramp their youthful limbs;
And the rocks around I've open'd,
That the sun at rising, setting,
May give freshness to their cheeks.
So they lie in rest and quiet,
In the bliss of happy dreams."
So they lay; and still, beside them,

Lay the dog in peaceful slumber,
Never whimpering in his sleep.

Years came on, and years departed;
Till at last the young men waken'd;
And the wall, so strongly fasten'd,
Now had fallen into ruin,
Crumbled by the touch of ages.
Then Iamblichus, the youngest,
And the goodliest of them all,
Seeing that the shepherd trembled,
Said, "I pray you now, my brothers,
Let me go to seek provision;
I have gold, my life I'll venture,
Tarry till I bring you bread."
Ephesus, that noble city,
Then, for many a year, had yielded
To the faith of the Redeemer,
Jesus. (Glory to his name!)

And he ran unto the city;
At the gate were many warders,
Armed men on tower and turret,

But he pass'd them all unchalleng'd;
To the nearest baker's went he,
And in haste demanded bread.

"Ha! young rogue," exclaimed the baker,
"Surely thou hast found a treasure;
That old piece of gold betrays thee!
Give me, or I shall denounce thee,
Half the treasure thou hast found."

And Iamblichus denied it;
But the baker would not listen,
Brawling till the watch came forward.
To the king they both were taken;
And the monarch, like the baker,
But a higher right asserting,
Claim'd to share the treasure too.

But at last the wondrous story,
Which the young man told the monarch,
Proved itself by many tokens.
Lord was he of that same palace,
Whither he was brought for judgment;
For he show'd to them a pillar,

In the which, a stone when loosen'd
Led unto a treasure chamber,
Heap'd with gold and costly jewels.
Straightway came in haste his kindred,
All his clan came thronging round him,
Eager to advance their claim;
Each was nearer than the other.
And Iamblichus, the blooming,
Young in face, and form, and feature,
Stood an ancestor among them.
All bewilder'd heard he legends
Of his son and of his grandsons,
Fathers of the men before him.
So amazed he stood and listen'd,
Patriarch in his early manhood;
While the crowd around him gather'd,
Stalwart men, and mighty captains,
Him, the youngest, to acknowledge
As the founder of their race!
And one token with another
Made assurance doubly certain;
None could doubt the wondrous story
Of himself and of his comrades.

Shortly, to the cave returning,
King and people all go with him,
And they saw him enter in.
But no more to king or people,
Did the Chosen reappear.
For the Seven, who long had tarried—
Nay, but they were eight in number,
For the faithful dog was with them—
Thenceforth from the world were sunder'd.
The most blessed angel Gabriel,
By the will of God Almighty,
Walling up the cave for ever,
Led them unto Paradise.

A.

THE CASTLE ON THE MOUNTAIN.

There stands an ancient castle
On yonder mountain height,
Where, fenced with door and portal,
Once tarried steed and knight.

But gone are door and portal,
And all is hush'd and still;
O'er ruin'd wall and rafter
I clamber as I will.

A cellar with many a vintage
Once lay in yonder nook;
Where now are the cellarer's flagons,
And where is his jovial look?

No more he sets the beakers
For the guests at the wassail feast;
Nor fills a flask from the oldest cask
For the duties of the priest.

No more he gives on the staircase
The stoup to the thirsty squires,
And a hurried thanks for the hurried gift
Receives, nor more requires.

For burn'd are roof and rafter,
And they hang begrimed and black;
And stair, and hall, and chapel,
Are turn'd to dust and wrack.

Yet, as with song and cittern,
One day when the sun was bright
I saw my love ascending
The slopes of yon rocky height;

From the hush and desolation
Sweet fancies did unfold,
And it seem'd as they had come back again,
The jovial days of old.

As if the stateliest chambers
For noble guests were spread,
And out from the prime of that glorious time,
A youth a maiden led.

And, standing in the chapel,
  The good old priest did say,
"Will ye wed with one another?"
  And we smil'd and we answer'd "Yea!"

We sung, and our hearts they bounded
  To the thrilling lays we sung,
And every note was doubled
  By the echo's catching tongue.

And when, as eve descended,
  The hush grew deep and still,
And the setting sun looked upward
  On that great castled hill;

Then far and wide, like lord and bride,
  In the radiant light we shone—
It sank; and again the ruins
  Stood desolate and lone!

M.

THE WATER-MAN.

This ballad cannot be claimed as one of Goethe's original compositions, it being a very close translation of an old Danish ballad, entitled "The Mer-man, and Marstig's Daughter." As, however, it appears in all the collections, and has often been quoted as a favourable specimen of Goethe's skill in assuming the simple style of the popular Northern ballads, we have deemed it advisable to give a version.

"Oh, mother! rede me well, I pray;
How shall I woo me yon winsome May?"

She has built him a horse of the water clear,
The saddle and bridle of sea-sand were.

He has donn'd the garb of a knight so gay,
And to Mary's Kirk he has ridden away.

He tied his steed to the chancel door,
And he stepp'd round the Kirk three times and four.

He has boune him into the Kirk, and all
Drew near to gaze on him, great and small.

The priest he was standing in the quire;—
"What gay young gallant comes branking here?"

The winsome maid, to herself said she,
"Oh, were that gay young gallant for me!"

He stepp'd o'er one stool, he stepp'd o'er two;
"Oh, maiden, plight me thine oath so true!"

He stepp'd o'er three stools, he stepp'd o'er four;
"Wilt be mine, sweet May, for evermore?"

She gave him her hand of the drifted snow—
"Here hast thou my troth, and with thee I'll go."

They went from the Kirk with the bridal train,
They danced in glee, and they danced full fain;

They danced them down to the salt-sea strand,
And they left them standing there, hand in hand.

"Now wait thee, love, with my steed so free,
And the bonniest bark I'll bring for thee."

And when they passed to the white, white sand,
The ships came sailing on to the land;

But when they were out in the midst of the sound,
Down went they all in the deep profound!

Long, long on the shore, when the winds were high,
They heard from the waters the maiden's cry.

I rede ye, damsels, as best I can—
Tread not the dance with the Water-Man!

M.

THE DANCE OF DEATH.

THE warder looked down at the dead of night
  On the graves where the dead were sleeping,
And, clearly as day, was the pale moonlight
  O'er the quiet churchyard creeping.
One after another the gravestones began
To heave and to open, and woman and man
  Rose up in their ghastly apparel!

Ho, ho for the dance!—and the phantoms outsprung
  In skeleton roundel advancing,
The rich and the poor, and the old and the young,
  But the winding-sheets hinder'd their dancing.
No shame had these revellers wasted and grim,
So they shook off the cerements from body and limb,
  And scattered them over the hillocks.

They crooked their thigh bones, and they shook their
    long shanks,
  And wild was their reeling and limber;

And each bone as it crosses, it clinks and it clanks,
Like the clapping of timber on timber.
The warder he laughed, tho' his laugh was not loud;
And the Fiend whispered to him—" Go, steal me the shroud
Of one of these skeleton dancers."

He has done it! and backward with terrified glance,
To the sheltering door ran the warder;
As calm as before looked the moon on the dance,
Which they footed in hideous order.
But one and another retiring at last,
Slipped on their white garments and onward they passed,
And a hush settled over the greensward.

Still, one of them stumbles and tumbles along,
And taps at each tomb that it seizes;
But 'tis none of its mates who has done it this wrong,
For it scents its grave-clothes in the breezes.
It shakes the tower gate, but *that* drives it away,
For 'twas nailed o'er with crosses—a goodly array—
And well was it so for the warder!

It must have its shroud—it must have it betimes—
  The quaint Gothic carving it catches;
And upwards from story to story it climbs,
  And scrambles with leaps and with snatches.
Now woe to the warder, poor sinner, betides!
Like a spindle-legged spider the skeleton strides
  From buttress to buttress, still upward!

The warder he shook, and the warder grew pale,
  And gladly the shroud would have yielded!
The ghost had its clutch on the last iron rail,
  Which the top of the watch-tower shielded.
When the moon was obscured by the rush of a cloud,
One! thundered the bell, and unswathed by a
    shroud,
  Down went the gaunt skeleton crashing!

M.

THE FAIREST FLOWER.

THE LAY OF THE CAPTIVE EARL.

THE EARL.

I KNOW a floweret passing fair,
  And for its loss I pain me;
Fain would I hence to seek its lair,
  But for these bonds that chain me.
Ah, heavy, heavy is my cheer,
For till I came a prisoner here,
  That flower was ever near me.

All round the castle's beetling steep,
  I let my glances wander;
But cannot from the dizzy keep
  Descry it, there or yonder.
Oh, he who'd bring it to my sight,
Or were he knave, or were he knight,
  Should be my friend for ever!

THE ROSE.

I blossom bright thy lattice near,
And hear what thou hast spoken;
'Tis me—brave, ill-starred cavalier—
The Rose, thou wouldst betoken!
Thy spirit spurns the base, the low,
And 'tis the queen of flowers, I know,
That in thy bosom reigneth.

THE EARL.

All honour to thy purple cheer,
From swathes of verdure blowing;
Well may'st thou be to maidens dear,
As gold or jewels glowing.
Thy wreaths adorn the fairest face,
Yet art thou not the flower, whose grace
In solitude I pine for.

THE LILY.

A haughty place usurps the rose,
And haughtier still doth covet;
But where the lily meekly blows,
Some gentle eye will love it.

The heart that's warm and fond and true,
And pure as mine, when bathed in dew,
  Must value me the highest.

THE EARL.

Ah, pure and true of heart am I,
  And free from sinful failing,
Yet must I here a captive lie,
  My loneliness bewailing.
I see the symbol fair in you
Of many maidens pure and true,
  Yet know a something dearer.

THE CARNATION.

That may thy warder's garden show
  In me, the bright carnation,
Else would the old man tend me so
  With loving adoration?
In perfect round my petals meet,
And lifelong are with scent replete,
  And with the loveliest colour.

THE EARL.

The sweet carnation none may slight,
  It is the gardener's pleasure;

Now he unfolds it to the light,
  Now shields from it his treasure.
But no—the flower for which I pant,
No rare, no brilliant charms can vaunt,
  'Tis ever meek and lowly.

THE VIOLET.

Concealed and drooping I retreat,
  Nor willingly had spoken,
But now my silence, since 'tis meet,
  It shall at length be broken.
If I be that which fills thy thought,
How must I grieve, that I may not
  To thee waft all my odours!

THE EARL.

I love the violet, indeed,
  So modest in perfection,
So gently sweet—yet more I need,
  To soothe my heart's dejection.
To thee alone the truth I'll speak,
Not on this rock, so bare and bleak,
  Is to be found my darling.

Earth's truest wife, in yonder glen,
  Is wandering by the river;
Till I, her lord, am free again,
  She'll sigh and weep for ever.
When a blue floweret by that spot
She plucks, and says—FORGET-ME-NOT,
  Here in my cell I feel it.

Yes, when two hearts are twined, love's might
  Is felt, whate'er the distance;
So I, within this dungeon's night,
  Cling ever to existence.
And when my heart is nigh distraught,
If I but say—FORGET-ME-NOT,
  Hope burns again within me!

M.

THE PARIAH.

I.

THE PARIAH'S PRAYER.

HEAR me, Brama, bending lowly!
  All from thee derive their being;
Therefore art thou just and holy!
  Is it, Lord, of thy decreeing,
That the Brahmins, high-estated,
  Only should thy bounty gather,
  Only dare to call thee, Father,
When us too thou hast created?

We are noble, Lord, in nothing!
  Woe, and want, and labour pain us;
What all others shun with loathing,
  Is the food that must sustain us.
When the scorn of caste is loudest,
  All we'd bear without repining,
4

  Were thy face toward us shining,
For thou canst rebuke the proudest.

Therefore, Lord, hear my entreaty!
  Raise me from this foul defilement,
Or a Saviour send, in pity,
  For the work of reconcilement.
Didst thou not a Bayaderé
  Lift from wretchedness to glory?
  Yea, we Pariahs have a story,
Giving comfort to the weary.

II.

THE PARIAH'S LEGEND.

Water from the sacred Ganges,
To bring water from the river,
Goes the noble Brahmin's wife.
She was chaste, and pure, and lovely;
High, immaculate, and honoured,
And of sternest justice he.
Daily from the sacred river

Does she fetch the pleasant water;
Not in pitcher nor in vessel,
For she hath no need of these.
Rises of itself the water,
Rolled into a ball of crystal,
To the stainless heart and hand
(Such the power of perfect virtue
Innocence without a shadow),
And she bears it to her home.

This day comes she in the morning,
Praying, to the flood of Ganges,
Bending lightly o'er the stream;
There she sees, as in a mirror,
From the heaven above reflected,
Floating in the liquid ether,
Such a glorious apparition!
Image of a youth, created
By the thought of the Almighty,
As a form of perfect beauty.
On the wondrous vision gazing,
Feels she straight a new sensation
Thrill throughout her inmost being;
Fascinated still she lingers,

Lingers with a secret longing;
Wishes it would pass, but ever
Floats the image back again.
In amazement, in confusion,
Stoops she to the flowing Ganges,
Trying, with her trembling fingers,
From the stream a ball to fashion.
But alas, the spell is broken!
For the holy water shuns her,
Seems to shrink as she approaches,
Whirling swiftly from her hands.

Nerveless drop her arms, she totters;
Scarce her fainting limbs can bear her,
Scarce she knows the pathway homewards;
Shall she fly, or shall she tarry?
Thought forsakes her; help and counsel
Are to her that day denied.

So she comes before her husband.
And he looks—his look is judgment!
Silently the sword he seizes,
Leads her to the hill of terrors,
Where adulterers meet their doom.

How can she, the wife, resist him?
What extenuation offer,
Guilty, knowing not her crime?

With the bloody sword yet dripping,
Homeward to his silent dwelling
Went the inexorable man.
Then his son came forth to meet him—
"Whose that blood? O father, father!"
"Blood of an adulteress!" "Never!
On the blade it has not stiffened,
As adulterous blood would do.
Fresh as from the wound 'tis running.
Mother, mother! O come hither!
Unjust was my father never,
What is this that he hath done?"

"Boy, be silent! *hers* the blood is!"
"Whose?" "Be silent!" "O my mother!
Is it then my mother's blood?
What's her crime? I will be answer'd!
Say, what evil hath she done?
Here—the sword!—Lo, now I grasp it!
Thou mightst slay thy wife unchallenged,

But my mother shalt thou not!
Wives through fire their husbands follow,
Children must avenge their mothers!
As the flames unto the widow,
Is the sword unto the son!"

"Hold thy hand!" exclaimed the father,
"Yet there's time; O hasten, hasten;
Join the head unto the body,
Touch it with the sword of vengeance,
And she'll follow thee alive!"

Rushing, breathless—what beholds he,
Stretched upon the hill of terror?
Bodies of two slaughter'd women,
And their heads are lying near.

Half distracted, blind, and dizzy,
His dear mother's head he seizes,
Does not even stay to kiss it,
Joins it to the nearest body:
Pointing then the sword of vengeance,
Piously completes the spell.

Riseth straight a ghastly figure!
From the dear lips of his mother,
Sweet as ever, nowise altered,
Comes this terrible bewail:

"Son, O son! what fatal rashness!
Yonder lies thy mother's body,
Near it is the head polluted
Of a wretched woman, victim
To the just avenging sword.
Me hast thou in hideous union
Blent for ever with her body!
Wise in will, but wild in doing,
Must I move among the spirits.
Yea, that godlike apparition,
Which the eye might blameless look on,
Which the brain might blameless think on,
To the heart becomes a torment,
Stirring passionate desire!

"Still that image must beset me!
Sometimes rising, sometimes falling,
Sometimes bright, and sometimes darken'd,
Such is mighty Brama's will.

He it was who sent the vision,
Floating on its angel pinions,
Radiant face and form so graceful,
God-created in its beauty,
For my trial and temptation;
Since from heaven we may be tempted,
If the Gods decree it so.
So must I, a sad Brahmina,
With my head to heaven pertaining,
Feel the gross and earthly passion
Of the Pariah evermore!

"Go, my son, unto thy father!
Be of comfort! Let no penance,
Dull remorse, or hope of merit,
Through a weary expiation,
Drive him to the wilderness.
Go ye forth among the people,
And, so long as speech remaineth,
Tell, O tell the meanest creature,
That him also Brama hears!

"For with Him there is no meanness.
In His sight are all men equal.
Be he leper, be he outcast,

Be he sunk in want and sorrow,
Be he desolate, heart-broken,
Be he Brahmin, be he Pariah—
Whosoever prays for mercy,
He shall have it, he shall find it,
When he turns his face to heaven.
Thousand eyes are watching yonder,
Thousand ears are ever listening,
Everything to God is known.

"When I pass before his footstool,
Me beholding, thus distorted
By a vile transfiguration,
Surely will the Father pity.
Yet my curse may be a blessing,
Unto you, my son, and many.
For, in humble adoration,
Meekly shall I strive to utter,
What the higher sense inspires;
Then, in frenzied adjuration,
Shall I tell him all the passion,
That is raging in this bosom
Thought and impulse, will and weakness—
Mystery of mysteries!"

III.

THE PARIAH'S THANKSGIVING.

Mighty Brama! I adore thee,
Maker thou of all creation;
And I dare to come before thee,
With my lowly supplication.

No respect for race thou showest,
Giving unto each a token,
E'en to us, the meanest, lowest,
Are the words of comfort spoken.

Thou hast heard that woman's story,
Thou hast heard her cruel sentence.
Lord! that art enshrined in glory,

THE CAVALIER'S CHOICE.

This lively little ballad occurs in one of Goethe's Operas, very charming compositions, which probably are less read than they deserve. It is not altogether original, being evidently founded on a popular Scottish ditty, called indiscriminately "Captain Wedderburn's Courtship," or "The Laird of Roslin's Daughter," in which precisely the same questions are propounded and answered. Truth compels us to say that, in point of merit, the superiority lies with the Scottish ballad. This being a case of disputed property, or rather commonty, the translator has allowed himself more license in rendering than has been used in any other instance in the present collection.

It was a gallant cavalier
  Of honour and renown,
And all to seek a ladye-love
  He rode from town to town.
Till at a widow-woman's door
  He drew the rein so free;
For at her side the knight espied
  Her comely daughters three.

Well might he gaze upon them,
  For they were fair and tall;
Ye never have seen fairer maids,
  In bower nor yet in hall.
Small marvel if the gallant's heart
  Beat quicker in his breast:
'Twas hard to choose, and hard to lose—
  How might he wale the best?

"Now, maidens, pretty maidens mine,
  Who'll rede me riddles three?
And she who answers best of all
  Shall be mine own ladye!"
I ween they blush'd as maidens do,
  When such rare words they hear—
"Now speak thy riddles, if thou wilt,
  Thou gay young cavalier!"

What's longer than the longest path?
  First tell ye that to me;
And tell me what is deeper yet,
  Than is the deepest sea?
And tell me what is louder far,
  Than is the loudest horn?

And tell me what hath sharper point,
Than e'en the sharpest thorn?

"And tell me what is greener yet,
Than greenest grass on hill?
And tell me what is crueller
Than a wicked woman's will?"
The eldest and the second maid,
They mus'd and thought awhile;
But the youngest she looked upward,
And spoke with merry smile:

"O, love is surely longer far,
Than the longest paths that be;
And hell, they say, is deeper yet,
Than is the deepest sea;
The roll of thunder is more loud,
Than is the loudest horn;
And hunger it is worse to bear
Than sharpest wound of thorn;

"The copper sweat is greener yet,
Than is the grass on hill;

And the foul fiend he is crueller
  Than any woman's will!"
He leapt so lightly from his steed,
  He took her by the hand;
"Sweet maid, my riddles thou hast read,
  Be lady of my land!"

The eldest and the second maid,
  They pondered and were dumb,
And there, perchance, are waiting yet
  Till another wooer come.
Then, maidens, take this warning word,
  Be neither slow nor shy,
But always, when a lover speaks,
  Look kindly, and reply.

A.

AN AUTUMN NIGHT'S DREAM.

Come, list, and the tale of a Count I will sing,
Who dwelt in the castle up here, sirs,
Where to-night the old rafters so merrily ring,
As we taste of his grandson's good cheer, sirs.
The Count had been long in the Saracen land,
And well knew the Moslem his terrible brand;
When he sprung from his steed at his gateway, and scann'd
The home of his fathers, the walls they were there,
But of servants and furniture empty and bare.

"So, so! my good Count, now you're fairly at home,
Matters look rather chilly and scowling;
The winds at their will through the windows roam,
From chamber to corridor howling.
A cheery look out on a wild autumn night!
Well! I've spent many such in more dolorous plight,
But still came the morning, and all was made right!"

So down on a truckle he laid him, and soon
He was dropping to sleep by the light of the moon.

For a while all was silent; but hark! what is that?
Like a scratching his truckle bed under!
"Oh, it's only the stir of some foraging rat;
If he hunts up a crumb there, I'll wonder."
But ha! at the feet of the travel-tired knight,
What is standing now? Lo! 'tis the tiniest wight,
A smart little dwarf, with a lamp for a light,
Long beard, and keen eyes with a glittering gleam!
The Count, if he sleeps not, to slumber doth seem.

"To sport it up here we have always been free,
Since the place was deserted by you so,
And thinking you still were abroad, sir, why, we
Had intended this evening to do so.
And with your permission, our people will bring
To this hall, which is spacious enough for a ring,
The bonny wee bride that has wedded our king!"
"The hall's at your service, my small friend, for me!"
Said the Count, dreaming on in a quaint reverie.

Then into the chamber, from under the bed,
  Three cavaliers mounted came prancing,
And behind them a troop of small elfin-folk sped,
  To fife and to clarion dancing;
Then carriage on carriage, with trappings so gay—
You only will see such a princely array,
At a great monarch's court on some festival day.
  At last came the bride in a carriage of sheen,
  Encircled by nobles escorting their Queen.

Now off through the hall they all scamper, and there
  In a twinkling they're station'd around it;
So ready's each dwarf with his Lilliput fair,
  To frisk it, and foot it, and bound it.
Then the fiddling, and fifing, and strumming begin,
Such whirling, and twirling, and skirling, and din,
Such giggling, and wriggling, through thick and
    through thin!
  The Count, as he looks from his truckle by fits,
  Believes he must surely be losing his wits.

And now come a patter, and clatter, and roar
  Of chairs. and of tables, and benches,

And each mannikin straight, for the banquet in store,
By his sweetheart his small self intrenches.
Then in come the sausage, the ham, and the chine,
Roast-meat, fish, and fowl, all so small and so fine,
And round and round circles the best of old wine;
They rattle and prattle for ever so long,
Then all disappear with a chorus of song.

And if I'm to tell what further befell,
A truce to your shouting and laughter!
What the Count saw in little enacted so well
He largely partook of thereafter;
The trumpets, the singing, the festival gay,
The coaches, the horsemen, the bridal array,
The crowds of blithe vassals all thronging to pay
To the bride her due honour; it was so of old,
And the same we were gladden'd this day to behold.

A. M.

THE PAGE AND MAID OF HONOUR;

OR, EFFECTS AT A DISTANCE.

THE Queen's in the hall where the torches are bright,
And the courtiers at faro are playing:
She signs to her Page—" I've forgotten to-night,
My purse with the gold for the paying.
Go fetch it; my cipher it bears for a mark,
It lies on the edge of the table."
And forth goes the youth, through the galleries dark,
As speedily as he was able.

The prettiest damsel that waits on the Queen,
Was lemonade daintily sipping,
When, somehow or other, the goblet so green
O'erflow'd at the touch of her lipping.
Ah me, what a pity! a splendid new dress
Quite spoiled by the juice from the chalice!
So up rose the damsel, in utmost distress,
And sped through the halls of the palace.

The Page coming back, in a corridor dim,
  Encounter'd the fugitive maiden;
None knew, save Dan Cupid—'twas patent to him—
  How tenderly both hearts were laden.
Of course, when a meeting occurs of the kind,
  It is vain the emotions to smother;
There was nobody near, and Dan Cupid is blind;
  So they heartily kiss'd one another.

Then up to her chamber ascended the May,
  To pay her fresh court to the Graces;
While the Page to the Queen threaded deftly his way,
  Through furbelows, flounces, and laces.
No sooner Her Majesty did him espy,
  Than, sharp as the Shebaite lady,
The lemonade stains on his vest caught her eye;
  She quite understood them already.

Then beckon'd she straight to the Mistress of Court,
  "Come here, and I'll show you a wonder;
You lately maintain'd more in earnest than sport,
  That the flesh kept the spirit quite under;
That mystical union was only a dream,
  That nothing exists save the Real;

That the stars, in their courses, are but what they
seem,
And their influence wholly ideal.

"Observe, my good Countess; there happen'd but
now,
A mischance to a maiden of honour;
And my Page, who just then was far distant, I vow,
Is mark'd by the stains that are on her!
Now this is an evidence, startling, though new,
Which surely should finish our quarrel,
And as they have gain'd me the triumph o'er you
Let them both have a change of apparel."

THE FALSE LOVER.

It was a gallant wild and free,
  From France he came, this rover,
And oft a poor young girl had he
  Caress'd and sworn to love her,
And fondled her, and press'd, and woo'd,
And toy'd as bridegroom only should,
  And in the end forsook her.

And hearing this, that nut-brown maid
  Was crazed and broken-hearted;
She laugh'd, and wept, and swore, and pray'd,
  And so her soul departed.
That hour a horror fell on him,
A crawling terror shook each limb,
  And on his horse he bounded.

With bloody spurs and visage pale,
  He dash'd on fast and faster,

Now here, now there, up hill, down dale,
  But no peace can he master;
Seven days, seven nights, he rides amain,
Through lightning, thunder, wind, and rain,
  And torrents fierce and swelling.

Through lightning-flash and tempest din
  On to a ruin rides he,
Ties up his horse and creeps within,
  And from the storm-blast hides he;
And as he gropes through darkness grim,
The earth falls inward under him,
  And down—down—down, he tumbles.

Reviving from the shock, he sees
  Three tapers faintly glancing,
He scrambles after them, but these
  Three tapers keep advancing;
Sideways, along, up stairs and down,
Through passages long, gaunt, and brown,
And crumbling vaults they lead him.

At once he stands within a hall
  Where countless guests are meeting,

Their hollow eyes give one and all
  A grim and ghastly greeting;
He sees his leman down below,
Array'd in garments white as snow,
  She turns—— M.

THE KING IN THULE.

A King there was in Thule,
  Kept troth unto the grave;
The maid he loved so truly
  A goblet to him gave.

And ever set before him
  At banquet was the cup;
And saddening thoughts came o'er him,
  Whene'er he took it up.

When Death with him had spoken,
  His treasures rang'd he there,
And all, save one dear token,
  He gifted to his heir.

Once more to royal wassail
  His peers he summon'd all;
Around were knight and vassal
  Throng'd in his father's hall.

Then rose the grand old Rover,
  Again the cup drain'd he,
And bravely flung it over
  Into the welt'ring sea.

He saw it flashing, falling,
  And settling in the main,
Heard Death unto him calling—
  He never drank again!

A.

THE MAGICIAN'S APPRENTICE.

HUZZAH, huzzah! His back is fairly
  Turned about, the wizard old;
And I'll now his spirits rarely
  To my will and pleasure mould!
His spells and orgies—ha'n't I
  Marked them all aright?
And I'll do wonders, sha'n't I?
  And deeds of mickle might.
      Hear ye! hear ye!
      Hence! your spritely
      Office rightly,
      Featly showing!
      Toil, until with water clear, ye
      Fill the bath to overflowing!

Ho, thou battered broomstick! take ye
  This old seedy coat and wear it—
Ha, thou household drudge! I'll make ye
  Do my bidding; ay, and fear it.

Don of legs a pair, now;
  A head too, for the nonce!
To the river there, now
  Bear the pail at once!
      Hear ye! hear ye!
      Hence! your spritely
      Office rightly,
      Featly showing!
      Toil, until with water clear, ye
      Fill the bath to overflowing.

See, 'tis off—'tis at the river
  In the stream the bucket flashes;
Now 'tis back—and down, or ever
  You can wink, the burden dashes.
Again, again, and quicker!
  The floor is in a swim,
And every stoup and bicker
  Is running o'er the brim.
      Stop, now stop!
      You have granted
      All I wanted.
      Stop! Od rot it!

Running still? I'm like to drop!
What's the word? I've clean forgot it!

Oh, the word, so strong and baleful,
To make it what it was before!
There it skips with pail on pailful—
Would thou wert a broom once more!
Still new streams he scatters,
Round and ever round me—
Oh, a hundred waters,
Rushing in, confound me!
No—no longer,
Can I brook it!
I'll rebuke it!
Vile abortion!
Woe is me, my fears grow stronger,
What grimacing, what contortion!

Wilt thou, offspring of the devil,
Drench the house in hellish funning?
Even now, above the level
Of the door, the water's running.
Stop, wretch! won't you hear me?
You for this shall pay.

Only you come near me!
  Stop, broom, stop, I say!
    Stop, I tell you,
    I'll not bear it,
    No, I swear it!
    Let me catch you,
    And upon the spot I'll fell you
    With my hatchet, and despatch you.

Back it comes—will nought prevent it?
  If I only tackle to thee,
Soon, O Kobold! thou'lt repent it,
  When the steel goes crashing thro' thee.
Bravely struck, and surely!
  There it goes in twain;
Now I move securely,
  And I breathe again!
    Woe and wonder!
    As it parted,
    Straight up started,
    'Quipped aright,
    Goblins twain that rush asunder.
    Help, O help, ye powers of might!

Deep and deeper grows the water
  On the stairs and in the hall,
Rushing in with roar and clatter—
  Lord and master, hear me call!
Ah, here comes the master—
  Sore, sir, is my strait;
I raised this spirit faster
  Far than I can lay't.
    "Broom, avaunt thee!
    To thy nook there!
    Lie, thou spook, there!
    Only answer,
    When for mine own ends I want thee,
    I, the master necromancer!"

M.

DOLEFUL LAY OF THE WIFE OF ASAN AGA.

This beautiful poem, purporting to be a translation from the Morlachian, was first printed in Herder's admirable collection of ballads; translated into German from almost every European language, and published under the title of Volkslieder. The fine poetic instinct of Goethe was signally displayed in this composition; for although, as Mickiewicz has observed (*Les Slaves*, tome i, p. 323, Paris, 1849), he had to divine the import of the poem across three bad translations, and was at the same time ignorant of the Slavic language, he produced a perfect version, having instinctively detected and avoided the faults of the previous translators.

What is yon so white beside the greenwood?
Is it snow, or flight of cygnets resting?
Were it snow, ere now it had been melted;
Were it swans, ere now the flock had left us.
Neither snow nor swans are resting yonder,
'Tis the glittering tents of Asan Aga.
Faint he lies from wounds in stormy battle;
There his mother and his sisters seek him,
But his wife hangs back for shame, and comes not.

When the anguish of his hurts was over,
To his faithful wife he sent this message—
"Longer 'neath my roof thou shalt not tarry,
Neither in my court nor in my household.

When the lady heard that cruel sentence,
'Reft of sense she stood, and rack'd with anguish:
In the court she heard the horses stamping,
And in fear that it was Asan coming,
Fled towards the tower, to leap and perish.

Then in terror ran her little daughters,
Calling after her, and weeping sorely,
"These are not the steeds of Father Asan;
Tis our uncle Pintorovich coming!"

And the wife of Asan turned to meet him;
Sobbing, threw her arms around her brother.
"See the wrongs, O brother, of thy sister!
These five babes I bore and must I leave them?"

Silently the brother, from his girdle,
Draws the ready deed of separation,

Wrapp'd within a crimson silken cover.
She is free to seek her mother's dwelling—
Free to join in wedlock with another.

When the woeful lady saw the writing,
Kiss'd she both her boys upon the forehead,
Kiss'd on both the cheeks her sobbing daughters;
But she cannot tear herself for pity
From the infant smiling in the cradle!

Rudely did her brother tear her from it,
Deftly lifted her upon a courser,
And in haste, towards his father's dwelling,
Spurr'd he onward with the woeful lady.

Short the space; seven days, but barely seven—
Little space I ween—by many nobles
Was the lady—still in weeds of mourning—
Was the lady courted in espousal.

Far the noblest was Imoski's cadi;
And the dame in tears besought her brother—
"I adjure thee, by the life thou bearest,

Give me not a second time in marriage,
That my heart may not be rent asunder
If again I see my darling children!"

Little reck'd the brother of her bidding,
Fix'd to wed her to Imoski's cadi.
But the gentle lady still entreats him—
"Send at least a letter, O my brother!
To Imoski's cadi, thus imploring—
I, the youthful widow, greet thee fairly,
And entreat thee, by this self-same token,
When thou comest hither with thy bridesmen,
Bring a heavy veil, that I may shroud me
As we pass along by Asan's dwelling,
So I may not see my darling orphans."

Scarcely had the cadi read the letter,
When he call'd together all his bridesmen;
Boune himself to bring the lady homewards,
And he brought the veil as she entreated.

Jocundly they reach'd the princely mansion,
Jocundly they bore her thence in triumph;
But, when they drew near to Asan's dwelling,

Then the children recognized their mother,
And they cried, "Come back unto thy chamber—
Share the meal this evening with thy children!"
Then she turn'd her to the lordly bridegroom—
"Pray thee, let the bridesmen and their horses
Halt a little by the once-loved dwelling,
Till I give these presents to my children."

And they halted by the once-loved dwelling,
And she gave the weeping children presents,
Gave each boy a cap with gold embroider'd,
Gave each girl a gay and costly garment,
And with tears she left a tiny mantle
For the helpless baby in the cradle.

These things mark'd the father, Asan Aga,
And in sorrow call'd he to his children—
"Turn again to me, ye poor deserted;
Hard as steel is now your mother's bosom;
Shut so fast, it cannot throb with pity!"
Thus he spoke; and when the lady heard him,
Pale as death she dropp'd upon the pavement;
And the life fled from her wretched bosom,
As she saw her children turning from her.

A.

MISCELLANEOUS POEMS.

MIGNON.

Knowest thou the land where the pale citron grows,
And the gold orange through dark foliage glows?
A soft wind flutters from the deep-blue sky,
The myrtle blooms, and towers the laurel high.
Knowest thou it well?
O there with thee!
O that I might, my own belov'd one, flee!

Knowest thou the house? On pillars rest its beams,
Bright is its hall, in light one chamber gleams,
And marble statues stand, and look on me—
What have they done, thou hapless child, to thee?
Knowest thou it well?
O there with thee!
O that I might, my lov'd protector, flee!

Knowest thou the track that o'er the mountain goes,
Where the mule threads its way through mist and
snows,
Where dwelt in caves the dragon's ancient brood,
Topples the crag, and o'er it roars the flood.
Knowest thou it well?
O come with me!
There lies our road—oh, father, let us flee!

M.

NECTAR-DROPS.

When Minerva, bent to favour
Him she cherish'd most, Prometheus,
Brought a chalice brimm'd with nectar
Down from heaven, to work a blessing
On the men he had created,
And inspire them with devotion
For the arts that deal with beauty;
Fleet of foot, she clove the ether,
That sire Jove might not espy her;

And the golden chalice trembled,
And some drops—not many were they—
Fell upon the emerald meadow.

Came the bees, and settling swiftly,
Suck'd their sweets with busy ardour;
Came the butterfly, as eager
To imbibe a droplet also;
Even the unshapely spinner
Crawl'd anear, and sucked with fervour.

Blessed was the draught they gather'd,
They and other tiny insects;
For they now, with men, contribute
Unto Art, that highest power!

M.

PROMETHEUS.

The following poem is part of a fragmentary drama, which Goethe never completed. The metre of the original, formed on the classical model, has been somewhat altered in the translation, for reasons similar to those which have been already assigned.

Curtain thy heavens, thou Jove, with clouds and mist,
And, like a boy that moweth thistles down,
Unloose thy spleen on oaks and mountain-tops;
Yet canst thou not deprive me of my earth,
Nor of my hut, the which thou didst not build,
Nor of my hearth, whose little cheerful flame
Thou enviest me!

I know not aught within the universe
More slight, more pitiful than you, ye Gods!
Who nurse your majesty with scant supplies
Of offerings wrung from fear, and mutter'd prayers,
And needs must starve, were't not that babes and
    beggars
Are hope-besotted fools!

When I was yet a child, and knew not whence
My being came, nor where to turn its powers,
Up to the sun I bent my wilder'd eye,
As though above, within its glorious orb,
There dwelt an ear to listen to my plaint,
A heart, like mine, to pity the oppress'd.

Who gave me succour
Against the Titans in their tyrannous might?
Who rescued me from death—from slavery?
Thou!—thou, my soul, burning with hallow'd fire,
Thou hast thyself alone achieved it all!
Yet didst thou, in thy young simplicity,
Glow with misguided thankfulness to him,
That slumbers on in idlesse there above!

I reverence thee?
Wherefore? Hast thou ever
Lighten'd the sorrows of the heavy-laden?
Thou ever stretched thy hand, to still the tears m
Of the perplexed in spirit?
Was it not
Almighty Time, and ever-during Fate—
My lords and thine—that shaped and fashion'd me
Into the MAN I am?

Belike it was thy dream,
That I should hate life—fly to wastes and wilds,
For that the buds of visionary thought
Did not all ripen into goodly flowers?

Here do I sit, and mould
Men after mine own image—
A race that may be like unto myself,
To suffer, weep; to enjoy, and to rejoice;
And, like myself, unheeding all of thee!

M.

THE GOBLET.

In my hands I held a brimming goblet,
Sculptured quaintly by the carver's cunning,
Quaff'd with eager lips the strong nepenthe,
So at once to drown all care and anguish.

Then came Amor in and found me sitting,
And he smiled a smile of serious sweetness,
As in pity of my foolish purpose.

"Friend, I know a vessel nobler, fairer
Worthy all your soul in it to bury;
Say what guerdon, if to thee I give it,
Fill it for thee with a rarer nectar?"

Oh, he kept his promise, and how truly!
Lida, when with thy dear love he bless'd me—
Me, that for thy sake had long been pining.

When I clasp thy beauties to my bosom,
And from thy fond lips, so fond and faithful,
Drink the balm of long long stored affection,
Thus entranced, I commune with my spirit.

"No; has never God, save Amor, fashion'd
Vessel such as this, nor e'er possessed it!
Forms so glorious ne'er were shaped by Vulcan,
With his finest soul-enprompted mallet.

"On the leaf-clad mountains may Lyæus
With his fauns, the hoariest, the sagest,
Cull the clusters of the daintiest savour,
Yea, may guide the mystic fermentation,
Draughts like this not all his skill can furnish!"

M.

MAHOMET'S SONG

THIS also is a fragment of an intended drama, of which Goethe has described the outline. After an elaborate explanation of his plan, he says, "This sketch long occupied my mind; for, according to my custom, I was obliged to let the conception perfect itself before I commenced the execution. All that genius, through character and intellect, can exercise over mankind, was therein to be represented, and what it gains and loses in the process. Several of the songs to be introduced in the drama were rapidly composed; the only one remaining of them, however, is the *Mahomet's Gesang*. This was to be sung by Ali in honour of his master, at the apex of his success, just before the change resulting from the poison."

Ho! the spring that bursts
From the mountain-height,
Joyous and bright
As the gleam of a star!
High o'er the clouds
In the rifts of the rocks,
'Neath the bare brushwood,
Its youth was nursed
By spirits of good.

Fresh as a boy
He dances down,
Down from the clouds,
On the marble rocks,
And back to the sky
He shouts.

Through the jagged clefts
He chases the mottled stones along,
And, with a leader's vanward tread,
He sweeps his brother rills
Along with him.

Down in the vale below
Flowers bud beneath his tread,
And, nourish'd by his breath,
The meadow lives.
Yet shady vale detains him not,
Nor any flowers that twine
Caressing round his knees,
And woo him with fond eyes:
On to the plain he speeds his course,
Winding in snaky bends.

Streamlets nestle
To his waters. Now he marches
To the champaign, silver-shining,
And the champaign shines with him,
And the rivers of the champaign,
And the streamlets of the mountains,
Shout to him, and cry out, "Brother!
Brother, take thy brothers with thee,
With thee to thine ancient father,
To the eternal Ocean,
Who with outstretch'd arms awaits us,
Arms which, ah! in vain are open,
To embrace his yearning children;
For the hungry sand consumes us
In the dreary desert; yonder
Sun drinks up our blood; a mountain
To a marish dams us! Brother,
Take thy brothers of the champaign,
Take thy brothers of the mountain,
With thee, with thee, to thy sire."

Come, come all!
And now swells he

Statelier. The banded rivers
Bear their monarch high aloft!
And, along in triumph rolling,
Names he gives to regions; cities
Grow amain beneath his feet.

On and ever on he rushes;
Spire and turret fiery-crested,
Marble palaces, the creatures
Of his wealth, he leaves behind.

Pine-built houses bears the Atlas
On his giant shoulders. O'er his
Head a thousand pennons rustle,
Floating far upon the breezes,
Tokens of his majesty.

And so beareth he his brothers,
And his treasures, and his children,
To their primal sire expectant,
All his bosom throbbing, heaving
With a wild tumultuous joy.

M.

THE ARTIST'S MORNING SONG.

My dwelling is the Muses' home—
  What matters it how small?
And here, within my heart, is set
  The holiest place of all.

When, waken'd by the early sun,
  I rise from slumbers sound,
I see the ever-living forms
  In radiance group'd around.

I pray, and songs of thanks and praise
  Are more than half my prayer,
With simple notes of music, tuned
  To some harmonious air.

I bow before the altar then,
  And read, as well I may,
From noble Homer's master-work,
  The lesson for the day.

He takes me to the furious fight,
  Where lion-warriors throng;
Where god-descended heroes whirl
  In iron cars along.

And steeds go down before the cars;
  And round the cumber'd wheel,
Both friend and foe are rolling now,
  All blood from head to heel!

Then comes the champion of them all,
  Pelides' friend is he,
And crashes through the dense array,
  Though thousands ten they be!

And ever smites that fiery sword
  Through helmet, shield, and mail,
Until he falls by craft divine,
  Where might could not prevail.

Down from the glorious pile he rolls,
  Which he himself had made,
And foemen trample on the limbs
  From which they shrank afraid.

Then start I up, with arms in hand,
  What arms the painter bears;
And soon along my kindling wall
  The fight at Troy appears.

On! on again! The wrath is here
  Of battle rolling red;
Shield strikes on shield, and sword on helm,
  And dead men fall on dead!

I throng into the inner press,
  Where loudest rings the din;
For there, around their hero's corpse,
  Fight on his furious kin!

A rescue! rescue! bear him hence
  Into the leaguer near;
Pour balsam in his glorious wounds,
  And weep above his bier!

And when from that hot trance I pass,
  Great Love, I feel thy charm;
There hangs my lady's picture near—
  A picture, yet so warm!

How fair she was, reclining there;
  What languish in her look!
How thrill'd her glance through all my frame,
  The very pencil shook.

Her eyes, her cheeks, her lovely lips,
  Were all the world to me;
And in my breast a younger life
  Rose wild and wantonly.

Oh! turn again, and bide thee here,
  Nor fear such rude alarms;
How could I think of battles more
  With thee within my arms!

But thou shalt lend thy perfect form
  To all I fashion best;
I'll paint thee first, Madonna-wise,
  The infant on thy breast.

I'll paint thee as a startled nymph,
  Myself a following faun;
And still pursue thy flying feet
  Across the woodland lawn.

With helm on head, like Mars, I'll lie
  By thee, the Queen of Love,
And draw a net around us twain,
  And smile on heaven above:

And every god that comes shall pour
  His blessings on thy head,
And envious eyes be far away
  From that dear marriage-bed!

A.

CUPID AS A LANDSCAPE PAINTER.

Once I sate upon a mountain,
Gazing on the mist before me;
Like a great grey sheet of canvass,
Shrouding all things in its cover,
Did it float 'twixt earth and heaven.

Then a child appear'd beside me,
Saying, "Friend, it is not seemly,
Thus to gaze in idle wonder,
With that noble breadth before thee.
Hast thou lost thine inspiration?
Hath the spirit of the painter
Died within thee utterly?"

But I turn'd and look'd upon him,
Speaking not, but thinking inly,
"Will he read a lesson now!"

"Folded hands," pursued the infant,
"Never yet have won a triumph.
Look! I'll paint for thee a picture
Such as none have seen before."

And he pointed with his finger,
Which like any rose was ruddy,
And upon the breadth of vapour
With that finger 'gan to draw.

First a glorious sun he painted,
Dazzling when I look'd upon it;
And he made the inner border
Of the clouds around it golden,
With the light rays through the masses
Pouring down in streams of splendour.
Then the tender taper summits
Of the trees, all leaf and glitter,
Started from the sullen void;
And the slopes behind them rising,
Graceful-lined in undulation,
Glided backwards one by one.
Underneath, be sure, was water;

And the stream was drawn so truly,
That it seem'd to break and shimmer,
That it seem'd as if cascading
From the lofty rolling wheel.

There were flowers beside the brooklet;
There were colours on the meadow—
Gold and azure, green and purple,
Emerald and bright carbuncle.
Clear and pure he work'd the ether
As with lapis-lazuli,
And the mountains in the distance
Stretching blue and far away—
All so well, that I, in rapture
At the second revelation,
Turn'd to gaze upon the painter,
From the picture which he drew.

"Have I not," he said, "convinced thee
That I know the painter's secret?
Yet the greatest is to come."

Then he drew with gentle finger,
Still more delicately pointed,

In the wood, about its margin,
Where the sun within the water
Glanced as from the clearest mirror,
Such a maiden's form!
Perfect shape in perfect raiment,
Fair young cheeks 'neath glossy ringlets,
And the cheeks were of the colour
Of the finger whence they came.

"Child," I cried, "what wondrous master
In his school of art hath form'd thee,
That so deftly and so truly,
From the sketch unto the burnish,
Thou hast finish'd such a gem?"

As I spoke, a breeze arising
Stirr'd the tree-tops in the picture,
Ruffled every pool of water,
Waved the garments of the maiden;
And, what more than all amazed me,
Her small feet took motion also,
And she came towards the station
Where I sat beside the boy.

So, when everything was moving,
Leaves and water, flowers and raiment,
And the footsteps of the darling—
Think you I remain'd as lifeless
As the rock on which I rested?
No, I trow—not I!

A.

THE VISIT.

To-day I thought to steal upon my darling,
But the door was closed of her apartments.
Of a key, however, I am master;
Noiselessly I glide within the doorway.

In the salon found I not the maiden,
Found the maiden not within the parlour,
But on tiptoe entering her chamber,
There I find her, sunk in graceful slumber,
In her robes, upon the sofa lying.

At her work had slumber overta'en her;
And the netting with the needles, rested
'Twixt the fair hands that hung crosswise folded.
Silently I sate me down beside her,
And awhile I mused, if I should wake her.

Awed me then the peace so sweet and holy,
Which upon her drooping eyelids rested:
On her lips abode a trustful quiet,
Beauty on her cheeks, the home of beauty;
And the tranquil movement of her bosom,
Show'd how innocent the heart that moved it.
All her limbs, so gracefully reposing,
Lay relax'd by sleep's delicious balsam:
There I sat enraptured, and the vision
Curb'd the impulse I had felt to wake her,
With a spell that close and closer bound me.

"Oh my love," I murmur'd, "and can slumber,
Which unmasks whate'er is false and formal,
Can he injure thee not, nor unravel
Ought to shake thy lover's fondest fancy?

"Thy dear eyes are closed, those eyes so tender—
Eyes, which only lifted are enchantment,
Those sweet lips, oh lips so sweet, they stir not,
Stir not nor for speech, nor yet for kisses!
All unloosen'd is the magic cincture
Of thine arms, that otherwhiles enclasp me,
And the hand, the dainty sweet companion
Of all best endearments, void of motion.
Were my thoughts of thee delusion merely—
Were my love for thee but self-deception,
I must now discern the truth, when Amor
Stands beside me thus, with eyes unbandaged."

Long while thus I sat, with heart elated,
Thinking of her worth and my devotion;
Sleeping, she with rapture so had fill'd me,
That I did not venture to awake her.

Placing softly down upon her table
Two pomegranates and two half-blown rosebuds,
Gently, gently glide I from the chamber.
When she opes her eyes, my own heart's darling,
And they rest upon my gift, with wonder

Will she muse, how such fond token ever
There should be, and yet her door unopen'd.

When to-night again I see my angel,
Oh, how she will joy, and twofold pay me,
For this tribute of my heart's devotion!

M.

A NIGHT THOUGHT.

I do not envy you, ye joyless stars,
Though fair ye be, and glorious to the sight—
The seaman's hope amidst the 'whelming storm,
When help from God or man there cometh none.
No! for ye love not, nor have ever loved!
Through the broad fields of heaven, the eternal hours
Lead on your circling spheres unceasingly.
How vast a journey have ye travell'd o'er,
Since I, upon the bosom of my love,
Forgot all memory of night or you!

M.

THE HAPPY PAIR.

It came and went so lightly,
  That pleasant summer rain;
Now see, dear wife, how brightly
  Laughs out our own domain.
Far, far into the distance
  The eager eye can roam,
But here is true existence,
  And here a happy home.

Down fly the pigeons cooing,
  The pretty graceful things!
So gentle in their wooing,
  Beside the fairy springs,
Where, gathering flowers together,
  A garland first I wove,
In bright and sunny weather,
  For thee, my only love!

Another wreath I plaited,
  As well rememberest thou,
That day when we were mated,
  And took the happy vow.
The world was all before us,
  To make or choose our way;
And years have stolen o'er us,
  Since that most blessed day.

The vow which then was spoken,
  A thousand times we've sealed,
By many a tender token,
  In thicket and in field;
On Alpine heights we've tarried,
  Together still were we;
Yea, Love for us hath carried
  His torch across the sea.

Contented and caressing,
  What could we wish for more?
God sent a greater blessing,
  We counted three and four;
Two more have joined the party,
  The little prattling elves!

But now they're strong and hearty,
  And taller than ourselves.

That story needs no telling;
  I see you looking down
On yonder new-built dwelling,
  Amid the poplars brown.
May all good angels guide him!
  For there our eldest sits,
His winsome wife beside him,
  Our own beloved Fritz.

How pleasant is the clatter,
  'Tis like a measured reel,
As yonder falling water
  Goes foaming o'er the wheel!
In many a song and ditty,
  Are miller's wives called fair;
But none are half so pretty
  As our dear daughter there.

Ah yes! I do not wonder
  Your eye should rest e'en now,

Upon the hillock yonder,
  Where dark the fir-trees grow.
There lie our babes together,
  Beneath the daisied sod;
But they have seen Our Father,
  And pray for us to God!

Look up! look up! for, glancing,
  The glint of arms appears;
And sound of music dancing,
  Strikes full upon my ears!
With trophies carried o'er them,
  In freedom's battle won,
Who walks so proud before them?
  'Tis Carl! it is my son!

The Rose he loves so dearly
  Is blushing on his breast—
Oh, wife! what follows nearly?
  Our hero's marriage-feast!
Methinks I see the wedding,
  The dancers and the glee,
And merriest measure treading,
  Our youngest children three!

The happy faces round us
  Will then recall the tide,
The blessed day that bound us
  As bridegroom and as bride.
Nay, tarry here and listen!
  Ere yet the year is done,
Our good old priest shall christen
  A grandchild and a son.

A.

LIMITS OF HUMANITY.

When the Creator,
The Great, the Eternal,
Sows with indifferent
Hand, from the rolling
Clouds, o'er the earth, His
Lightnings in blessing,
I kiss the nethermost
Hem of His garment,
Lowly inclining
In infantine awe.

For never against
The immortals, a mortal
May measure himself.
Upwards aspiring, if ever
He toucheth the stars with his forehead,
Then do his insecure feet
Stumble and totter and reel;
Then do the cloud and the tempest
Make him their pastime and sport.

Let him with sturdy
Sinewy limbs,
Tread the enduring
Firm-seated earth;
Aiming no further, than with
The oak or the vine to compare!

What doth distinguish
Gods from mankind?
This! Multitudinous
Billows roll ever
Before the Immortals,
An infinite stream.
We by a billow

Are lifted—a billow
Engulfs us—we sink,
And are heard of no more!

A little round
Encircles our life,
And races unnumber'd
Extend through the ages,
Link'd by existence's
Infinite chain.

M.

PHILINE'S SONG.

Sing not thus in notes of sadness
  Of the loneliness of night;
No! 'tis made for social gladness,
  Converse sweet, and love's delight.

As to rugged man his wife is
  For his fairest half decreed,
So dear night the half of life is,
  And the fairest half indeed.

Who could hail the day with pleasure,
  Which but interrupts our joys,
Scares us from our dreams of leisure
  With its glare and irksome noise?

But when night is come, and glowing
  Is the lamp's attemper'd ray,
And from lip to lip are flowing
  Love and mirth, in sparkling play;

When the fiery boy, that wildly
  Gambols in his wayward mood,
Calms to rest, disporting mildly,
  By some trivial gift subdued;

When the nightingale is trilling
  Songs of love to lovers' ears,
Which, to hearts with sorrow thrilling,
  Seem but sighs and waken tears;

How, with pulses lightly bounding,
  Leaps the heart to hear the bell,
Which, the hour of midnight sounding,
  Doth of rest and safety tell.

Then, dear heart, this comfort borrow
  In the long day's lingering light—
Every day hath its own sorrow,
  Gladness cometh with the night!

M.

THE

YOUTH AND THE MILL-STREAM.

YOUTH.

Pretty brooklet, gaily glancing
  In the morning sun,
Why so joyous in thy dancing?
  Whither dost thou run?
What is't lures thee to the vale?
Tell me, if thou hast a tale.

BROOK.

Youth! I was a brooklet lately,
  Wandering at my will;
Then I might have moved sedately;
  Now, to yonder mill,
Must I hurry, swift and strong,
Therefore do I race along.

YOUTH.

Brooklet, happy in thy duty,
  Nathless thou art free;
Knowest not the power of beauty
  That enchaineth me!
Looks the miller's comely daughter
Ever kindly on thy water?

BROOK.

Early comes she every morning,
  From some blissful dream;
And, so sweet in her adorning,
  Bends above my stream.
Then her bosom, white as snow,
Makes my chilly waters glow.

YOUTH.

If her beauty brings such gladness,
  Brooklet, unto thee,
Marvel not if I to madness
  Should enflamèd be.
O that I could hope to move her!
Once to see her is to love her.

BROOK.

Then careering—ah, so proudly!
  Rush I o'er the wheel,
And the merry mill speaks loudly,
  All the joy I feel.
Show me but the miller's daughter,
And more swiftly flows my water.

YOUTH.

Nay, but, brooklet, tell me truly,
  Feelest thou no pain,
When she smiles, and bids thee duly
  Go, nor turn again?
Hath that simple smile no cunning,
Brook, to stay thee in thy running?

BROOK.

Hard it is to lose her shadow,
  Hard to pass away;
Slowly, sadly, down the meadow,
  Uninspired I stray.
O, if I might have my will,
Back to her I'd hasten still!

YOUTH.

Brook! my love thou comprehendest;
Fare-thee-well awhile;
One day, when thou hither wendest,
May'st thou see me smile.
Go, and in thy gentlest fashion,
Tell that maiden all my passion?

A.

POESY.

When men were rude, and rough, and wild,
Jove sent down Law, and Art, and Knowledge,
To form on earth a kind of college,
And make the savage creatures mild.

But the poor Virtues, when they came,
Had nought to hide their nakedness,
Till Poesy the lack supplied,
And clothed them in her seemliest dress.

A.

THE WANDERER.

WANDERER.

YOUNG woman, may
God's blessing be upon thee,
And on the suckling babe
Upon thy breast!
Suffer me, here against the cliff,
Under the elm-tree's shade,
To lay my knapsack down,
And rest awhile beside thee.

WOMAN.

What business sends thee here,
Under the noonday heat,
Along the dusty road?
Wares from the city bring'st thou,
To sell about the country?
Thou smilest at my question?

WANDERER.

Wares from the city bring I none.
The evening air grows cool,

I pray you, fair young wife,
Show me the spring where you drink.

WOMAN.

You see the track there up the rocks,
Follow it. Right through the thicket,
'Twill lead you along to the cottage;
There do I dwell;—to the spring,
Where I drink.

WANDERER.

Signs of man's constructive hand
Among the bushes! Nature, thou,
Who dost with prodigality profuse,
Scatter thy handiworks abroad,
Didst never join these stones!

WOMAN.

Still higher up!

WANDERER.

An architrave half buried in the moss!
Man's shaping spirit has been busy here;
It has impress'd its seal upon the stone.

WOMAN.

On, stranger, farther still!

WANDERER.

Lo! An inscription 'neath my weary feet!
Not to be read! Ye have departed, too,
Ye deeply-graven characters, that should
Have testified your master's piety
To thousand generations yet to come.

WOMAN.

You startle, stranger,
At these old stones? There are
Many more such up yonder,
Close to my cottage.

WANDERER.

Up there?

WOMAN.

Yes.—Turn to the left,
And hold through the brushwood! Here!

WANDERER.

Ye Muses and ye Graces!

WOMAN.

This is my cottage.

WANDERER.

A Temple's ruins!

WOMAN.

Down at the side there
Bubbles the spring, where I drink.

WANDERER.

On flame-tipp'd wings
Thou hoverest o'er thy grave,
Oh Genius! Oh thou Immortal,
Above thee, tumbled in ruins,
Thy masterpiece lies!

WOMAN.

Wait, and I will fetch
A cup, that thou mayest drink.

WANDERER.

Around thy slender symmetry divine,
The ivy hath a garment wound.

Twin pillars, how ye lift
Your heads from out the wreck!
And thou, lone sister yonder, how dost thou,
With dusky lichen on thy sacred brows,
Look down, majestical in grief,
Upon the shatter'd fragments, at thy feet,
Which were thy sisters once!
Beneath the bramble's shade they lie,
With dust and rubbish strewn,
And over them the long rank spear-grass waves!
Nature, is't thus thou prizest
Thy masterpiece's masterpiece?
Dost thou, without relenting or remorse,
Thy sanctuary thus in ruins lay,
And sow it with the thistle and the thorn?

WOMAN.

How the boy sleeps!
Wilt rest within the cottage?
Or wilt thou, stranger, rather here
Sit in the open air?
'Tis cool! Here, take my boy,
Whilst I go fetch the water.
Sleep on, my darling, sleep!

WANDERER.

Delicious is thy rest.
Bathed in celestial health,
How tranquilly he breathes!
Thou, who hast, amid the relics
Of the sacred past, been born,
May its spirit dwell with thee!
He, who is by it environ'd,
Will, with pulses like a God's,
Taste of joy through all his days.
Thou pregnant germ, bloom on,
The bright and golden Spring's
Incomparable gem,
Outshining all thy mates!
And when thy wither'd petals drop,
Oh, from thy bosom then,
May the rich fruitage rise,
And ripen 'gainst the sun!

WOMAN.

God bless him! Is he still asleep?
Nothing have I, except a piece of bread,
With the fresh draught to offer you.

WANDERER.

Thanks, thanks!
How glorious are
The blossoms and the verdure everywhere!

WOMAN.

My husband from the field will soon be home.
Stay, friend, and join us at our evening meal.

WANDERER.

And you dwell here?

WOMAN.

Yes, here; within these walls.
It was my father, who the cottage built,
Of tiles and stones got from the ruins here.
And here we dwell.
He gave me to a husbandman,
And died within our arms.
And have you had a dainty sleep, my sweet?
How frolicsome he is, and full of play!
Ha, rogue!

WANDERER.

Oh, ever-budding Nature, thou
Dost frame all creatures to enjoy their life,
And all thy children, with maternal care,
Hast dower'd with an inheritance, a home.
High on the sculptured frieze the swallow builds,
Unconscious of the ornament she hides;
The caterpillar weaves her coil
Around the golden bough,
To make a winter lodgment for her brood;
And, 'midst the glorious ruins of the past,
Dost thou, oh man, for thy necessities
A cottage rear, and spend thy days in peace,
With graves beneath thy feet!
Thou happy wife, farewell!

WOMAN.

Thou wilt not stay?

WANDERER.

God keep thee, bless thy boy!

WOMAN.

Good luck attend thee!

WANDERER.

Whither leads the path
Across the mountain yonder?

WOMAN.

To Cuma.

WANDERER.

And how far off is that?

WOMAN.

'Tis good three miles.

WANDERER.

Farewell!
Oh Nature, guide my steps!
The stranger's wandering steps,
Where they may tread on graves
Of bygone days, that wear,
Transfigured in the mists of time,
A semblance nigh divine!
Oh lead him onward to some shelter'd spot,
Fenced from the icy North,
And where a stir of leaves

Averts the noonday beam!
And when at eve I come,
Back to my cottage home,
Which the sun's parting rays have tipp'd with
gold,
May such a wife be there, to welcome me,
My boy upon her arm!

M.

SONG

OF THE

SPIRITS OVER THE WATERS.

The soul of man,
It is like water;
From heaven it cometh,
To heaven it mounteth,
And then again,
Still interchanging
Evermore, returns to earth.

Aloft it shoots,
A star in brightness,
From the beetling
Wall of rock.
Then in waves
Of graceful vapour,
On the glistening
Basalt, dustlike
Falls, and touched, and
Touching lightly,
Like a veil
It showers down, softly
Whispering, to its craggy base.

Rocks rise up,
To stem back the torrent,
And madly from steep to steep
Headlong it dashes,
Plunging in foam
To the whirling abyss.

Anon with murmurs low
It winds and wimples on,
Along the meadowy vale,

And in the unruffled lake,
Heaven's stars their faces all
Contemplate, and are glad.

Wind is the water's
Favourite paramour;
Wind stirs the waves up
In foam from the deeps.

Man's spirit, oh how like
Art thou to the water!
Man's destiny, how like
Art thou to the wind!

M.

GANYMEDE.

Oh, what a glow
Around me in morning's
Blaze thou diffusest,
Beautiful spring!
With the rapture of love, but intenser,
Intenser, and deeper, and sweeter,
Nestles and creeps to my heart
The sensation divine
Of thy fervour eternal,
Oh, thou unspeakably fair!
Oh, in this arm
That I might enfold thee!

Alas! on thy bosom
I lay me, I pine,
And thy flowers, and thy greensward
Are press'd to my heart.
Thou coolest the fiery
Thirst of my bosom,

Dear breeze of morn!
Bear'st me the nightingale's
Fond adjuration,
Forth from the mists of the vale!
I come, I am coming!
Where art thou? oh where?

Aloft! thou art there!
See, where they sweep down,
The clouds, how they bend down,
Inclining to answer
The yearning of love!
Come to me! come!
Up to your bosom
Bear me on high!
Embraced and embracing
Up to thy bosom,
All-loving Sire!

M.

THE MUSAGETES.

Often in the winter midnight,
Pray'd I to the blessed Muses—
"Here is not the red of morning,
Tardy is the day in breaking;
Light for me, ye blessed Muses,
Light the lamp of inspiration,
That its mellow ray may serve me,
'Stead of Phœbus and Aurora!"
But they left me to my slumber,
Dull, and spiritless, and torpid;
And the morning's lazy leisure
Usher'd in a useless day.

Then when spring began to kindle,
Thus the nightingales I conjured—
"Sweetest nightingales, O warble,
Warble early at my window!
Wake me from the heavy slumber
That in magic fetters hold me!"

And the love-o'erflowing singers
Sang all night around my window
All their rarest melodies;
Kept awake the soul within me;
Gave me trances, aspirations,
Glimpses of divine emotion,
Soothing, melting, undefined.
So the night pass'd lightly over,
And Aurora found me sleeping,
Scarce I waken'd with the sun.

Lastly, came the glorious summer:
What aroused me then from dreaming,
At the earliest dawn of morning?
'Twas the buzzing of the flies!
They are touch'd by no compassion,
Ruthlessly they do their duty;
Though the half-awaken'd sleeper
Greets them with a malediction.
Unabash'd their clan they summon,
And the humming swarm is vocal,
And they banish from my eyelids,
All the luxury of sleep.

Straightway start I from my pillow,
Leave the close-beleaguer'd chamber,
Sally out to seek the Muses,
In the haunts to them are dearest.
And I find them 'neath the beeches,
Waiting for me, sometimes chiding,
For my over-long delay.
Thus I owe you, libelled insects,
Thanks for many hours of rapture.
Dullards may indeed abuse you,
Since you wake them to sensation;
But the poet ought to prize you,
And I thank you, as a poet,
Ranking you, beyond all others,
As the ushers to the Muse.

A.

THE CHURCH WINDOW.

THE Minster window, richly glowing,
With many a gorgeous stain and dye,
Itself a parable, is showing,
The might, the power of Poesy.

Look on it from the outer square,
And it is only dark and dreary;
Yon blockhead always views it there,
And swears its aspect makes him weary.

But enter once the holy portal—
What splendour bursts upon the eye!
There symbols, deeds, and forms immortal,
Are blazing forth in majesty.

Be thankful you, who have the gift
To read and feel each sacred story;
And O, be reverent when you lift
Your eyes to look on heavenly glory!

A.

LILI'S PARK.

THIS curious poem marks the period when Goethe, unfortunately for himself, broke off his engagement to Anna Schönemann, whom he has celebrated under the pseudonym of "Lili."

THERE'S no menagerie, I trow,
So varied as my Lili's now.
The strangest beasts she keeps therein,—
Heaven knows how she procured them all!
The wild, the tame, the thick, the thin,
The great, the middling, and the small.
O how they strut and swagger madly,
  And flap their close-clipp'd wings in vain!
Poor princes, metamorphosed sadly,
And doom'd to love's eternal pain.

Who the fairy? who the Circe?
  Is it Lili?—ask not me;
But be thankful for the mercy,
  If she is not known to thee

What a gabbling, what a squeaking!
  At the door she takes her stand,
  With the basket in her hand;
Then the herd comes wildly shrieking!
Trees and bushes, they are bending
  With the weight of songsters sweet;
Larger creatures, hither wending,
  Roll and grovel at her feet.
Such devotion! 'tis amazing!
  Saw ye ever such a rout?
E'en the fishes in the basin,
  Bob their stupid noses out!
Then her daily dole she scatters,
  With a look, that might ensnare
  Jove or Hermes, were they there,
Bent on less terrestrial matters.
What a gaping! what a biting!
What a wrestling! what a fighting!
What a coil with teeth and claws!
What a fight with bill and paws!
What a tumbling, thronging, snatching,
Each at other fiercely catching!
What a chasing and a racing,
  For the crumbs so loosely shed!

Ah! Enchantress Lili, placing
  But her hand upon the bread,
Gives it an ambrosial flavour,
Steeps it in celestial savour!

O, but her look! O, but her tone!
  "Pipi! Pipi!" you hear her crying;
And Jove's own eagle, from his throne,
  Would come before her, gently flying;
The turtle-doves of Aphrodite,
  Would answer gladly to her call;
And Juno's peacocks, not too flighty,
  Would stoop from the Olympian hall.
They could not help it, sage or silly,
If once they heard the voice of Lili!

And what has this enchantress done?
  A great wild bear, unlick'd and rude,
  She lured from out his native wood,
And made him move in unison
With other beasts that tamer be,
(Up to a certain point, d'ye see?)
For slightly savage still was he!

Alas! how gracious and how good
  Seem'd then to me that gentle warden!
She might have ask'd me for my blood,
  To nurture flowers within her garden.

"Ask'd *you?* Pray, sir, explain your riddle!"
  In brief, 'tis I that am the bear;
Not prone to dance to every fiddle,
  But surely tangled in a snare.
An apron-net was strong enough
  To make my capture quite complete;
A silken thread has brought the rough
  Half-savage Bruin to her feet.
The story I may tell hereafter—
To-day, I'm not disposed for laughter.

Well! I am standing, rather sulky,
  Within a corner; hear the screeching,
  And all the manifold beseeching,
Of creatures that are not so bulky.
I turn me round; a growl I utter,
  Then move as if to go away.
I cannot; so again I mutter,
  And in despite of self must stay.

Suddenly a fit of passion
  Comes upon me; wild I grow,
  And I hurry to and fro,
Snorting in most bear-like fashion!
"What! be treated like a hare?
  Made a fool of, and a noodle?
Like the wretched squirrel there,
  Or that meanest beast, her poodle!"
Rise the bristles on my back—
  "No! a slave I will not be!"
And I fly; but in my track,
  Every bush and every tree,
  Upstarts, seem to scoff at me!
O'er the bowling-green I scour,
  Slipping on the close-mown grass,
And a box-tree near the bower
  Grins derision as I pass!
Crashing thro' the deepest thicket,
  Now I try to leap the pale,
Since I cannot ope the wicket:
  Woe is me! alas, I fail!
I can neither climb nor vault;
Magic brings me to a halt;
Magic weighs me down like lead.

So, with aching limbs and head,
Plod I to a quiet glade,
Where a miniature cascade,
Fashion'd by some artist's cunning,
Over shells and stones is running.
There I roll, and pant, and blow,
  Whine and whimper in my pain;
With rare audience for my woe—
  Oreads of porcelain!

Ah, what sound, what voice divine,
  Comes upon my senses stealing,
With a strain so rich and fine,
  Calming every tortured feeling?
O, the bliss that music bringeth,
Lili in her arbour singeth!
"O matchless voice for ever dear!
  The very air grows warm around!
Ah, does she sing that I may hear?"
  And, quite distracted by the sound,
I trample down the shrubs and flowers,
  I burst into her loved retreat—
Be gracious, O ye heavenly powers;
  For lo—the bear is at her feet!

"Well! you *are* the drollest creature!
Quite a monster with that hair;
Shagged, ragged, grim in feature,
Yet so gentle for a bear."
With her foot my back caressing,
Me she sends to Paradise!
Never felt I such a blessing—
O that heavenly, heavenly pressing!
But there's calm within her eyes.
I kiss her shoes, I lick their sole,
As courteous as a bear may be,
And then, entranced beyond control,
I lay my head upon her knee.
She lets me do it: nay, she tickles
My ear in very sportive mood;
I feel as if a thousand prickles
Were running through my flesh and blood!
In ecstasy I try to purr,
Perhaps it had been wiser not;
For my attempt extorts from her—
"*Allons tout doux! eh la menotte!*
Et faites serviteur,
Comme un joli Seigneur."

So never does she cease her funning;
  The poor fond beast, so oft betray'd,
Yet plumes himself upon his cunning,
  And thinks that he has pleased the maid.
His abject homage was regarded;
Drop that, and he's at once discarded.

But O, she is a witch indeed!
  She carries still a vial precious,
  Fill'd with a balsam so delicious,
As shames the draught of Ganymede.
One drop of that, upon my tongue,
  She placed with her enchanting finger,
Then forthwith from the arbour sprung;
  I could not stay, I could not linger!
I still must follow in her train,
I seek, I tremble, turn again,
But will I have not of my own.
Sometimes I thought I might have flown;
But aye she stands beside the door;
She holds it open, trips before,
But gives me such a witching smile,
That, tho' I know her wonted wile,
I cannot leave her all the while!

Ye gods, of whom the ancients tell!
Witchcraft by you was always hated;
You might relieve me from this spell,
But you are dotards, or translated.
The rage for freedom stirs throughout my being:
I must be free! Myself will force my freeing!

A.

RETRIBUTION.

He that with tears did never eat his bread,
He that hath never lain through night's long hours,
Weeping in bitter anguish on his bed—
He knows ye not, ye dread celestial powers.
Ye lead us onwards into life. Ye leave
The wretch to fall; then yield him up, in woe,
Remorse, and pain, unceasingly to grieve;
For every sin is punish'd here below.

M.

THE WEDDING FEAST.

I CHANCED to walk, not long ago,
Into the village down below;
The people all were gaily drest,
They told me 'twas a marriage feast.

Within the dancing-room I found
Some sixty couples whirling round;
Each lass supported by her lad,
And every face was blithe and glad.

"A happy day, indeed!" I cried;
"But tell me, which may be the bride?"
The bumpkin answer'd with a stare—
"Lord, sir! I neither know nor care!

"Three nights have we been dancing here,
And tasting of her wedding cheer;
I merely came for fun and drinking,
About the bride I've not been thinking!"

If every man would speak the truth,
As freely as this honest youth,
His case would not—so ponder'd I—
Betoken singularity.

A.

PSYCHE.

The Muses, maiden sisters, chose
To teach poor Psyche arts poetic;
But, spite of all their rules æsthetic,
She never could emerge from prose.

No dulcet sounds escaped her lyre,
E'en when the summer nights were nigh;
Till Cupid came, with glance of fire,
And taught her all the mystery.

A.

THE

TREACHEROUS MAID OF THE MILL.

Lo! here is our comrade—he's racing along,
Ere day break his exercise taking;
Has he been to the chapel to hear matin-song?
With cold his poor bones must be aching!
The brook lies before him; barefooted he goes,
Through the ice-water manfully tearing!
What says he? An orison twang'd through his nose?
Ah no, my dear friend, he is swearing!

Alas! from a bed that he slyly bespoke,
He has started with wonderful vigour,
And, save for the sheltering folds of his cloak,
He would cut a most ludicrous figure.
Some impudent scoundrel has seized on his coat,
His vest, and his breeches, for payment;
And sent our poor friend, on the highway to trot,
Like Adam, in primitive raiment.

The reason? I'll tell you—he'll tell you, the dunce!
 For his shame is too plain to be hidden;
Down there at the mill, as in Paradise once,
 Grows fruit which is strictly forbidden.
Our friend has been poaching! Such dangerous trips
 End seldom except in vexation;
Let him in, give him liquor, and from his own lips
 Let us hear his absurd lamentation.

"In the amorous glance of the brown maiden's eye,
 No treachery did I discover;
She loved me, adored me—she said so; and I
 Was exceedingly pleased as her lover.
How could I imagine, while sweetly caress'd,
 What horrible thoughts she was hatching?
I was very content as she clung to my breast,
 Some hundreds of kisses despatching.

"It was pleasant enough, till the deep of the night,
 When I found myself, somehow or other,
Disrobed of my daily habiliments quite;
 Then the damsel shriek'd out for her mother!

Saint Paul! what a horrible rush was there then!
  Nay, listen, my dear friends, with patience—
A mother, a brother, of cousins full ten,
  Aunts, uncles, and other relations!

"Then a clamour arose might have waken'd the dead!
  Like tiger-cats fierce they were squalling!
'Her honour! her honour!' the women folk said;
  'Her virtue!' the strong knaves kept bawling.
And all this to me, an unfortunate youth,
  Who really was guiltless of sinning!
For a wiser than I had been baffled, in truth,
  Had he taken the odds for the winning.

"Her virtue! If Cupid is vigilant still,
  If his aim, as of yore, is as steady,
I rather imagine, that maid of the mill
  Knows some of his secrets already!
In short, sirs, they eagerly pounced on my dress,
  Coat, waistcoat, and breeches of kersey,
A fund of division for twenty, not less;
  That I saved my old cloak was a mercy!

"I leap'd on the floor; I struggled and swore,
To get out was my only endeavour;
And there stood the maiden, quite close to the door,
With a smile as enchanting as ever!
So frantic was I that the boldest gave way;
I cleft them, like hay-bands, asunder:
They let me go forth, in my simple array;
Save my cloak, there was nothing to plunder.

"You laugh, sirs, at this! well, I fairly must own,
No whit you're securer from pillage,
Should you leave the more elegant nymphs of the town,
To prowl after nymphs of the village.
Let women have lovers, as oft as they will,
And change, without any disclosure;
But never with scandal, like her of the mill,
Subject them to shameful exposure."

So told us his story, our shivering friend,
And we shouted in mirthful derision;
No grain of compassion had we to expend,
On a gallant in such a condition.

For richly deserves he sore penance to pay,
  The youth, who, from constancy falling,
Pays court to an innocent maiden by day,
  And at night sallies forth caterwauling!

A.

COPTIC SONG.

Howe'er they may wrangle, your pundits and sages,
  And love of contention infects all the breed,
All the philosophers, search through all ages,
  Join with one voice in the following creed:
  Fools from their folly 'tis hopeless to stay!
Mules will be mules, by the law of their mulishness;
Then be advised, and leave fools to their foolishness,
  What from an ass can be got but a bray?

When Merlin I question'd, the old Necromancer,
  As halo'd with light in his coffin he lay,
I got from the wizard a similar answer,
  And thus ran the burden of what he did say:

Fools from their folly 'tis hopeless to stay!
Mules will be mules, by the law of their mulishness;
Then be advised, and leave fools to their foolishness,
What from an ass can be got but a bray?

And up on the wind-swept peaks of Armenia,
And down in the depths, far hid from the day,
Of the temples of Egypt and far Abyssinia,
This, and but this, was the gospel alway:
Fools from their folly 'tis hopeless to stay!
Mules will be mules, by the law of their mulishness;
Then be advised, and leave fools to their foolishness,
What from an ass can be got but a bray?

M.

SONGS AND LYRICS.

THE MODERN AMADIS.

THEY kept me guarded close, while yet
A little tiny elf,
And so I sat, and did beget
A world within myself,
All I cared to see.

Golden fancy then unfurl'd
Endless sights to me,
And a gallant knight I grew;
Like the Prince Pipi,
Roam'd throughout the world.

Many a crystal palace saw,
  Many overthrew;
My far-flashing falchion hurled,
  Through the dragon's maw.
Ha! then I was a man!

Next I free'd in knightly wise
  The Princess Periban;
Oh, the wonder of her eyes,
  Smiling, as I woo'd
Her with hearted sighs!

Her kiss, it was ambrosial food,
  Glow'd like noble wine;
With love, oh, I was almost dead!
  A golden haze divine
She around her shed.

Who has torn her from my sight?
  Can no spell delay
That dear vision, stay her flight?
  Where her home, oh, say?
And thither, which the way?

M.

THE WILD ROSE.

A BOY espied, in morning light,
　　A little rosebud blowing;
'Twas so delicate and bright,
That he came to feast his sight,
　　And wonder at its growing.
Rosebud, rosebud, rosebud red,
　　Rosebud brightly blowing!

I will gather thee—he cried—
　　Rosebud brightly blowing!
Then I'll sting thee, it replied,
And you'll quickly start aside
　　With the prickle glowing.
Rosebud, rosebud, rosebud red,
　　Rosebud brightly blowing!

But he pluck'd it from the plain,
　　The rosebud brightly blowing!
It turned and stung him, but in vain—

He regarded not the pain,
Homewards with it going.
Rosebud, rosebud, rosebud red,
Rosebud, brightly blowing!

M.

THE BREEZE.

The mists they are scatter'd,
The blue sky looks brightly,
And Eolus looses
The wearisome chain!
The winds, how they whistle!
The steersman is busy—
Hillio-ho, hillio-ho!
We dash through the billows—
They flash far behind us—
Land, land, boys, again!

M.

THE COQUETTE.

O'ER the meadows tripp'd sweet Kitty,
  On a dewy morn in spring,
Like a lark, her blithesome ditty
  Gaily, lightly carolling,
    So la la! Le ralla.

Lubin, as she pass'd beside him,
  Offer'd two lambs for a kiss;
Roguishly awhile she eyed him,
  Tripp'd away, then caroll'd this,
    So la la! Le ralla.

Ribbons red young Colin proffers,
  Robin with his heart would wile,
But she mocks at all their offers,
  Singing, as she mounts the stile,
    So la la! Le ralla.

M.

SMITTEN.

THROUGH the wood as I was roaming,
  There a gentle youth I spied,
Piping sweetly in the gloaming,
  Till the rocks around replied,
      So la la!

And beside him down he drew me,
  Call'd me fair, and kiss'd me then.
Pipe once more! I said, and through me
  Thrill'd his music sweet again.
      So la la!

Now my peace is flown, and never
  Comes a smile into mine eye,
And within my ears for ever
  Rings that music and I sigh,
      So la la!

M.

JUST IN TIME.

WHEN Constance, fickle maid, forsook me,
For life or joy I ceased to care;
So to the river I betook me,
To finish all my sorrows there.

Upon the bank somehow I found me,
In dumb despair, my head a-spin,
And things went whirling round and round me,
I plunged—no, I was plunging in.

When hark! what was that sudden cry for?
I turn'd my head, to snatch a peep;
Oh, 'twas a voice to sigh and die for!
"Be careful, sir! The river's deep!"

And lo! a maid so fresh, so pretty,
A thrill through every vein I felt.
"Your name, your name, I pray you?" "Kitty."
At charming Kitty's feet I knelt.

"In death I had ere this been sleeping;
My life, I owe it all to you;
Oh, make your boon, then, worth the keeping,
And be its joy and blessing—do!"

And then I told her all my troubles,
Her eyelids dropp'd, she held her breath;
The kiss I gave, her kiss redoubles,
And now—my thoughts don't run on death.

M.

RESOLVE.

On, on, across the plains, and feel no dread!
Where not the boldest hath
Trod down a path, which thou may'st safely tread,
Make for thyself a path!

Still thou my heart, dear love! It will not break
Though bent awhile it be;
And if it needs must be, that it shall break,
It breaks not, love, with thee.

M.

TREASURE TROVE.

THROUGH the forest idly,
  As my steps I bent,
With a free and happy heart,
  Singing as I went.

Cowering in the shade I
  Did a floweret spy,
Bright as any star in heaven,
  Sweet as any eye.

Down to pluck it stooping,
  Thus to me it said,
"Wherefore pluck me only
  To wither and to fade?"

Up with its roots I dug it,
  I bore it as it grew,
And in my garden-plot at home
  I planted it anew;

All in a still and shady place,
  Beside my home so dear,
And now it thanks me for my pains,
  And blossoms all the year.

M.

IN ABSENCE.

And shall I then regain thee never?
  My beautiful! And art thou flown?
Still in mine ears resounds for ever
  Thy every word, thy every tone.

As through the air, when morn is springing,
  The wanderer peers in vain, to trace
The lark, that o'er him high is singing,
  Hid in the azure depth of space;

So, love, through field and forest lonely
  My sad eyes roam in quest of thee;
My songs are tuned to thee, thee only;
  Oh come, my own love, back to me!

M.

WHO'LL BUY A CUPID?

Of all the wares so pretty
That come into the city,
There's none are so delicious,
There's none are half so precious,
As those which we are bringing.
O, listen to our singing!
Young loves to sell! young loves to sell!
My pretty loves who'll buy?

First look you at the oldest,
The wantonest, the boldest!
So loosely goes he hopping,
From tree and thicket dropping,
Then flies aloft as sprightly—
We dare but praise him lightly!
The fickle rogue! Young loves to sell!
My pretty loves who'll buy?

Now see this little creature—
How modest seems his feature!
He nestles so demurely,
You'd think him safer surely;
And yet for all his shyness,
There's danger in his slyness,
The cunning rogue! Young loves to sell!
My pretty loves who'll buy?

Oh come and see this lovelet,
This little turtle-dovelet!
The maidens that are neatest,
The tenderest and sweetest,
Should buy it to amuse 'em,
And nurse it in their bosom.
The little pet! Young loves to sell!
My pretty loves who'll buy?

We need not bid you buy them,
They're here, if you will try them.
They like to change their cages;
But for their proving sages

No warrant will we utter—
They all have wings to flutter.
The pretty things! Young loves to sell!
Such beauties! Come and buy!

A.

A CALM AT SEA.

Lies a calm along the deep,
  Like a mirror sleeps the ocean,
And the anxious steersman sees
  Round him neither stir nor motion.

Not a breath of wind is stirring,
  Dread the hush as of the grave—
In the weary waste of waters
  Not the lifting of a wave.

M.

HUNTSMAN'S EVENING SONG.

In silence sad, from heath to hill
With rifle slung I glide,
But thy dear shape, it haunts me still,
It hovers by my side.

Across the brook, and past the mill,
I watch thee gaily fleet;
Ah, does one shape, that ne'er is still,
E'er cross thy fancy, sweet?

'Tis his, who, tortured by unrest,
Roams ever to and fro,
Now ranging east, now ranging west,
Since forced from thee to go.

And yet at times the thought of thee,
Like moonlight in a dream,
Doth bring, I know not how, to me
Content and peace supreme.

M.

THE LOVELY NIGHT.

From the cot, where softly sleeping
  Lies my bosom's love, I go,
And with noiseless footstep creeping,
  Thread the dusky wood, when lo!
Bursts the moon through glade and greenwood,
  Soft the herald zephyrs play,
And the waving birches sprinkle
  Sweetest incense on my way.

How I revel in the coolness
  Of this beauteous summer night!
Stilly dreaming here the fulness
  Of the panting soul's delight!
Words can paint not what my bliss is,
  Yet, kind heaven, I'd yield to thee
Nights a thousand, fair as this is,
  Would my love give one to me!

M.

FIRST LOVE.

Oh, who will bring me back the days,
  So beautiful, so bright!
Those days when love first bore my heart
  Aloft on pinions light?
Oh, who will bring me but an hour
  Of that delightful time,
And wake in me again the power
  That fired my golden prime?

I nurse my wound in solitude,
  I sigh the livelong day,
And mourn the joys, in wayward mood,
  That now are pass'd away.
Oh, who will bring me back the days
  Of that delightful time,
And wake in me again the blaze
  That fired my golden prime?

M.

SEPARATION.

I THINK of thee whene'er the sun is glowing
Upon the lake;
Of thee, when in the crystal fountain flowing
The moonbeams shake.

I see thee when the wanton wind is busy,
And dust-clouds rise;
In the deep night, when o'er the bridge so dizzy
The wanderer hies.

I hear thee when the waves, with hollow roaring,
Gush forth their fill;
Often along the heath I go exploring,
When all is still.

I am with thee! Though far thou art and darkling,
Yet art thou near.
The sun goes down, the stars will soon be sparkling—
Oh, wert thou here!

A.

WITH AN EMBROIDERED RIBBON.

LITTLE flowerets, little leaflets,
Have they woven with fairy hand,
Playful sunny elves of springtide,
Lightly called at my command.

Zephyr, bear it on thy pinions,
Drop it on my darling's dress,
So she'll pass before the mirror
In her doubled loveliness.

She, of roses still the fairest,
Roses shall around her see;
Give me but one look, my dearest,
And I ask no more of thee.

Feel but what this heart is feeling—
Frankly place thy hand in mine—
Trust me, love, the tie which binds us
Is no fragile rosy twine.

M.

SECOND LIFE.

After life's departing sigh,
To the spots I loved most dearly
In the sunshine and the shadow,
By the fountain welling clearly,
Through the wood and o'er the meadow,
Flit I like a butterfly.

There a gentle pair I spy.
Round the maiden's tresses flying,
From her chaplet I discover
All that I had lost in dying,
Still with her and with her lover.
Who so happy then as I?

For she smiles with laughing eye;
And his lips to her he presses,
Vows of passion interchanging,
Stifling her with sweet caresses,

O'er her budding beauties ranging;
And around the twain I fly.

And she sees me fluttering nigh;
And beneath his ardour trembling,
Starts she up—then off I hover.
"Look there, dearest!" Thus dissembling,
Speaks the maiden to her lover—
"Come and catch that butterfly!"

A.

TO MY MISTRESS.

All that's lovely speaks of thee!
When the glorious sun appeareth,
'Tis thy harbinger to me:
Only thus he cheereth.

In the garden where thou go'st,
There art thou the rose of roses,
First of lilies, fragrant most
Of the fragrant posies.

When thou movest in the dance,
  All the stars with thee are moving,
And around thee gleam and glance,
  Never tired of loving.

Night!—and would the night were here!
  Yet the moon would lose her duty;
Though her sheen be soft and clear,
  Softer is thy beauty!

Fair, and kind, and gentle one!
  Do not moon, and stars, and flowers
Pay that homage to their sun,
  That we pay to ours?

Sun of mine, that art so dear—
  Sun, that art above all sorrow!
Shine, I pray thee, on me here
  Till the eternal morrow!

M.

TO LUNA.

Sister of the earliest light,
Type of loveliness in sorrow,
Silver mists thy radiance borrow,
Even as they cross thy sight.
When thou comest to the sky,
In their dusky hollows waken,
Spirits that are sad, forsaken,
Birds that shun the day, and I.

Looking downward far and wide,
Hidden things thou dost discover.
Luna! help a hapless lover,
Lift him kindly to thy side!
Aided by thy friendly beams,
Let him, through the lattice peeping,
Look into the room where, sleeping,
Lies the maiden of his dreams.

Ah, I see her! Now I gaze,
Bending in a trance Elysian,
And I strain my inmost vision,
And I gather all thy rays.
Bright and brighter yet I see
Charms no envious robes encumber;
And she draws me to her slumber,
As Endymion once drew thee.

A.

TO THE BETROTHED.

Hand in hand, and lip to lip, love!
  Swear, thou'lt still be true to me!
Fare thee well! By many a cliff, love,
  Lies my track across the sea.
But when, every danger over,
  Safe in port again we lie,
If apart from thee thy lover
  Can be happy, let me die!

Boldly dared is won already,
  Half my task is conquer'd quite;
Stars to me are sunlight steady,
  Cowards only feel 'tis night.
Were I near thee, idly musing,
  Sad my fancies still would be,
But o'er distant oceans cruising,
  Toil is sweet, for 'tis for thee!

Even now I see it glowing,
  That dear vale, where we shall stray,
By the river softly flowing,
  While the daylight hours decay.
Where the silver birch is sweeping,
  Where the beech's shadows fall,
Ah! and there a cottage peeping
  Sweetly forth amid them all.

M.

THE PARTING.

Let mine eye the farewell make thee,
  Which my lips refuse to speak;
Scorn me not, if, to forsake thee,
  Makes my very manhood weak.

Joyless in our joy's eclipse, love,
  Are love's tokens, else divine,
Cold the kisses of thy lips, love,
  Damp the hand that's locked in mine.

Once thy lip, to touch it only,
  To my soul has sent a thrill,
Sweeter than the violet lonely,
  Pluck'd in March-time by the rill.

Garlands never more I'll fashion,
  Roses twine no more for thee;
Spring is here, but, ah, my passion,
  Autumn dark has come for me!

M.

COMFORT IN TEARS.

How is it that thou art so sad
  When others are so gay?
Thou hast been weeping—nay, thou hast!
  Thine eyes the truth betray.

"And if I may not choose but weep,
  Is not my grief mine own?
No heart was heavier yet for tears—
  O leave me, friend, alone!"

Come join this once the merry band,
  They call aloud for thee,
And mourn no more for what is lost,
  But let the past go free.

"O, little know ye in your mirth,
  What wrings my heart so deep!
I have not lost the idol yet,
  For which I sigh and weep."

Then rouse thee and take heart! thy blood
  Is young and full of fire;
Youth should have hope and might to win,
  And wear its best desire.

"O, never may I hope to gain
  What dwells from me so far;
It stands as high, it looks as bright,
  As yonder burning star."

Why, who would seek to woo the stars
  Down from their glorious sphere?
Enough it is to worship them,
  When nights are calm and clear.

"Oh, I look up and worship too—
  My star it shines by day—
Then let me weep the livelong night
  The whilst it is away."

M.

THE SHEPHERD'S LAMENT.

Up yonder on the mountain,
 I dwelt for days together;
Look'd down into the valley,
 This pleasant summer weather.

My sheep go feeding onward,
 My dog sits watching by;
I've wander'd to the valley,
 And yet I know not why.

The meadow, it is pretty,
 With flowers so fair to see;
I gather them, but no one
 Will take the flowers from me.

The good tree gives me shadow,
 And shelter from the rain;
But yonder door is silent,
 It will not ope again!

I see the rainbow bending,
  Above her old abode,
But she is there no longer;
  They've ta'en my love abroad.

They took her o'er the mountains,
  They took her o'er the sea;
Move on, move on, my bonny sheep,
  There is no rest for me!

EVENING.

Peace breathes along the shade
Of every hill,
The tree-tops of the glade
Are hush'd and still;
All woodland murmurs cease,
The birds to rest within the brake are gone.
Be patient, weary heart—anon,
Thou too, shalt be at peace!

M.

TO BELINDA.

Why dost thou lure me to this garish pleasure,
This pomp of light?
Was I not happy in abundant measure,
In the lone night?

Shut in my chamber, when the moon was beaming,
Unseen I lay,
And, with its silver radiance round me streaming,
I dream'd away.

I dream'd of hours which golden joy was filling,
And I was blest,
For love, tumultuous love, even then was thrilling
Through all my breast.

Am I the same, treading with thee the dances
Of this bright hall,
Amid the whispering tongues and jealous glances
That round us fall?

No more Spring's sweetest flowers can claim my duty,
  Or charm my view;
Where thou art, darling, there are love and beauty
  And nature, too.

M.

LOVE'S DREAM.

Thou oft in dreams hast seen us stand
Before the altar hand in hand,
Thyself the bride, the bridegroom I.
Oft on thy lips, when none were watching,
I've hung, unnumber'd kisses snatching,
In hours of waking ecstasy.

The purest rapture that we cherish'd,
The bliss of hours so golden, perish'd
Even with the hour that saw it rise.
What recks that mine have been such blisses?
Fleeting as dreams are fondest kisses,
And like a kiss all pleasure dies.

M.

MAY SONG.

How gloriously gleameth
  All nature to me!
How bright the sun beameth,
  How fresh is the lea!

White blossoms are bursting
  The thickets among,
And all the gay greenwood
  Is ringing with song!

There's radiance and rapture
  That naught can destroy,
Oh earth, in thy sunshine,
  Oh heart, in thy joy!

Oh love! thou enchanter,
  So golden and bright—
Like the red clouds of morning
  That rest on yon height;—

It is thou that art clothing
  The fields and the bowers,
And everywhere breathing
  The incense of flowers!

Oh maiden! dear maiden!
  How well I love thee—
Thine eye, how it kindles
  In answer to me!

Oh, well the lark loveth
  Its song 'midst the blue;
Oh, gladly the flowerets
  Expand to the dew.

And so do I love thee;
  For all that is best,
I draw from thy beauty
  To gladden my breast!

And all my heart's music
  Is thrilling for thee!
Be evermore blest, love,
  And loving to me!

M.

DEPRESSION.

Roses, ah, how fair ye be!
  Ye are fading, dying!
Ye should with my lady be,
  On her bosom lying;
All your bloom is lost on me,
  Here despairing, sighing.

Oh, the golden dreams I nursed,
  Ere I knew thy scorning,
When I pour'd my passion first,
  And at break of morning,
Pluck'd the rosebuds, ere they burst,
  For thy breast's adorning!

Every fruit and floweret rare,
  To thy feet I bore it,
Fondly knelt, to see thee there,
  Bending fondly o'er it,

Gazing on thy face so fair,
  To revere, adore it.

Roses, ah! how fair ye be!
  Ye are fading, dying!
Ye should with my lady be,
  On her bosom lying;
All your bloom is lost on me,
  Here despairing, sighing.

M.

TO THE MOON.

Flooded are the brakes and dell
  With thy phantom light,
And my soul receives the spell
  Of thy mystic might.

To the meadow dost thou send
  Something of thy grace,
Like the kind eye of a friend,
  Beaming on my face.

Echoes of departed times
  Vibrate on mine ear,
Joyous, sad, like spirit chimes,
  As I wander here.

Flow, flow on, thou little brook;
  Ever onward go!
Trusted heart, and tender look,
  Left me even so.

Richer treasure earth has none
  Than I once possessed—
Ah, so rich, that when 'twas gone,
  Worthless was the rest.

Little brook! adown the vale,
  Rush, and take my song;
Give it passion, give it wail,
  As thou leap'st along.

Sound it in the winter night,
  When thy streams are full;
Murmur it when skies are bright,
  Mirror'd in the pool.

Happiest he of all created,
  Who the world can shun,
Not in hate, and yet unhated;
  Sharing thought with none,

Save one faithful friend; revealing,
  To his kindly ear,
Thoughts like these, which, o'er me stealing,
  Make the night so drear.

A.

THE SPIRIT'S GREETING.

High on the beetling turret old,
  The hero's ghost doth stand,
And blesses thus the galley bold,
  Is sailing from the strand.

"Lo, once these sinews were as steel,
  This heart beat wild and high,
In field and fight the foremost knight,
  My cup was never dry.

"One half my life was storm and strife,
  One half was peaceful ease;
And thou, thou tiny mortal bark,
  Sail gladly with the breeze!"

M.

WITH A GOLDEN NECKLACE.

Accept, dear maid, this little token,
  A supple chain that fain would lie,
And keep its tiny links unbroken
  Upon a neck of ivory.

Pray, then, exalt it to this duty,
  And change its humbleness to pride!
By day, it will adorn your beauty,
  By night, 'tis quickly laid aside.

But if another hand should proffer
  A chain of weightier, closer kind,
Think twice ere you accept the offer;
  For there are chains will not unbind.

A.

ON THE LAKE.

THIS little poem was composed during a tour in Switzerland in 1775. Several others in this series belong to the same period, being that when Goethe's passion for Anna Elizabeth Schönemann, the Lili of his poems, was at its height.

FREE is my heart from every weight,
No care now cumbers me;
O Nature, thou art grand and great,
And beautiful to see!
Our boat goes dancing o'er the wave,
The rudder-track behind;
And yonder rise the mountains brave;
Blow fresh, blow fresh, thou wind!

What is this? Mine eyes are burning!
Golden dreams, are ye returning?
Vanish, golden though you be!
Here is love and life for me.

The spray of the water
Like star-showers is blown;
The mists they draw upwards,
From each mountain throne,
The morning wind ripples
The reach of the bay,
And the trees in the mirror
Are dancing alway.

A.

THE WANDERER'S NIGHT SONG.

Child of heaven, that soothing calm
On every pain and sorrow pourest,
And a doubly-healing balm
Find'st for him, whose need is sorest,
Oh, I am of life aweary!
What availeth its unrest—
Pain that findeth no release,
Joy that at the best is dreary?
Gentle peace,
Come, oh come into my breast!

M.

TO LINA.

Lina, rival of the linnet,
  When these lays shall reach thy hand,
Please transfer them to the spinnet,
  Where thy friend was wont to stand.

Set the diapason ringing,
  Ponder not the words you see,
Give them utterance by thy singing,
  Then each leaf belongs to thee.

With the life of music fill them;
  Cold the written verses seem,
That, would Lina deign to trill them,
  Might be trancing as a dream.

A.

TO A GOLDEN HEART.

PLEDGE of departed bliss,
Once gentlest, holiest token!
Art thou more faithful than thy mistress is,
That ever I must wear thee,
And on my bosom bear thee,
Although the bond that knit her soul with mine is
broken?
Why shouldest thou prove stronger;
Short are the days of love, and wouldst thou make
them longer?

Lili! in vain I shun thee!
Thy spell is still upon me.
In vain I wander through the distant forests strange,
In vain I roam at will
By foreign glade and hill,
For, ah! where'er I range,
Beside my heart, the heart of Lili nestles still!

Like a bird that breaks its twine,
Is this poor heart of mine:
It fain into the summer bowers would fly,
And yet it cannot be
Again so wholly free;
For always it must bear
The token which is there,
To mark it as a thrall of past captivity.

A.

SORROW WITHOUT CONSOLATION.

O, WHEREFORE shouldst thou try
The tears of love to dry?
Nay, let them flow!
For didst thou only know,
How barren and how dead
Seems everything below,
To those who have not tears enough to shed,
Thou'dst rather bid them weep, and seek their comfort so.

A.

WELCOME AND DEPARTURE.

To horse!—away, o'er hill and steep!
  Into the saddle blithe I sprung;
The eve was cradling earth to sleep,
  And night upon the mountains hung.
With robes of mist around him set, 1
  The oak like some huge giant stood,
While with its hundred eyes of jet,
  Peer'd darkness from the tangled wood.

Amidst a bank of clouds, the moon
  A sad and troubled glimmer shed;
The wind its chilly wings unclosed,
  And whistled wildly round my head.
Night framed a thousand phantoms dire,
  Yet did I never droop nor start;
Within my veins what living fire!
  What quenchless glow within my heart!

We met; and from thy glance a tide
  Of stifling joy flow'd into me:
My heart was wholly by thy side,
  My every breath was breathed for thee.
A blush was there, as if thy cheek
  The gentlest hues of spring had caught,
And smiles so kind for me!—Great powers!
  I hoped, yet I deserved them not!

Bu morning came to end my bliss;
  A long, a sad farewell we took.
What joy—what rapture in thy kiss,
  What depth of anguish in thy look!
I left thee, sweet! but after me,
  Thine eyes through tears look'd from above;
Yet to be loved—what ecstasy!
  What ecstasy, ye gods, to love!

M.

EARLY SPRING.

Come ye so early,
  Days of delight?
Making the hillside
  Blithesome and bright?

Merrily, merrily,
  Little brooks rush,
Down by the meadow,
  Under the bush.

Welkin and hilltop,
  Azure and cool;
Fishes are sporting
  In streamlet and pool.

Birds of gay feather
  Flit through the grove,
Singing together,
  Ditties of love.

Busily coming
  From moss-cover'd bowers,
Brown bees are humming,
  Questing for flowers.

Lightsome emotion,
  Life everywhere;
Faint wafts of fragrance
  Scenting the air.

Now comes there sounding
  A sough of the breeze,
Shakes through the thicket,
  Sinks in the trees.

Sinks, but returning,
  It ruffles my hair;
Aid me this rapture,
  Muses, to bear!

Know ye the passion
  That stirs in me here?
Yestre'en at gloaming
  Was I with my dear!

A.

THE BLISS OF ABSENCE.

'Tis sweet for him, the livelong day that lies,
Wrapt in the heaven of his dear lady's eyes,
  Whose dreams her image blesseth evermore.
Love knoweth not a sharper joy than this,
Yet greater, purer, nobler is the bliss,
  To be afar from her whom we adore!

Distance and Time, eternal powers, that be
Still, like the stars, o'erruling secretly,
  Cradle this tempest of the blood to peace.
Calm grows my soul, and calmer every hour,
Yet daily feels my heart a springing power,
  And daily finds my happiness increase.

All times she lives within my heart and brain,
Yet can I think of her without a pain,
  My spirit soars alway serene and free,
And, by the strength of its divine emotion,

Transforms its love to all a saint's devotion,
  Refines desire into Idolatry.

The lightest cloudlet that doth fleck the sky,
And floats along the sunshine airily,
  More lightly in its beauty floateth never,
Than doth my heart, with tranquil joy elate,
By fear untouch'd, for jealousy too great,
  I love, oh yes, I love—I love her ever!

M.

FROM THE MOUNTAIN.

If I, my own dear Lili, loved thee not,
  How should I joy to view this scene so fair!
And yet if I, sweet Lili, loved thee not,
  Should I be happy here or anywhere?

M.

LONGING.

What stirs in my heart so?
  What lures me from home?
What forces me outwards,
  And onwards to roam?
Far up on the mountains
  Lie cloudlets like snow;
O were I but yonder,
  'Tis there I must go!

Now by come the ravens
  So solemn and black;
I mingle among them,
  And follow their track:
By rock and by turret
  We silently glide;
Ah, there is the bower, where
  My lady doth bide!

She walks in the greenwood,
  That beautiful may;

Like a bird singing clearly,
  I drop on the spray.
She lists, and she lingers,
  And softly says she—
"How sweetly it singeth,
  It singeth for me!"

The sunset is gilding
  The peaks of the hill,
The day is declining,
  Yet tarries she still:
She follows the brooklet
  Through meadow and glade,
Till dark is the pathway,
  And lost in the shade.

Then, then I come down, as
  A swift-shooting star;
"What light glitters yonder,
  So near yet so far?"
Ere yet the amazement
  Hath passed from thee, sweet,
My quest it is ended
  I lie at thy feet!

A.

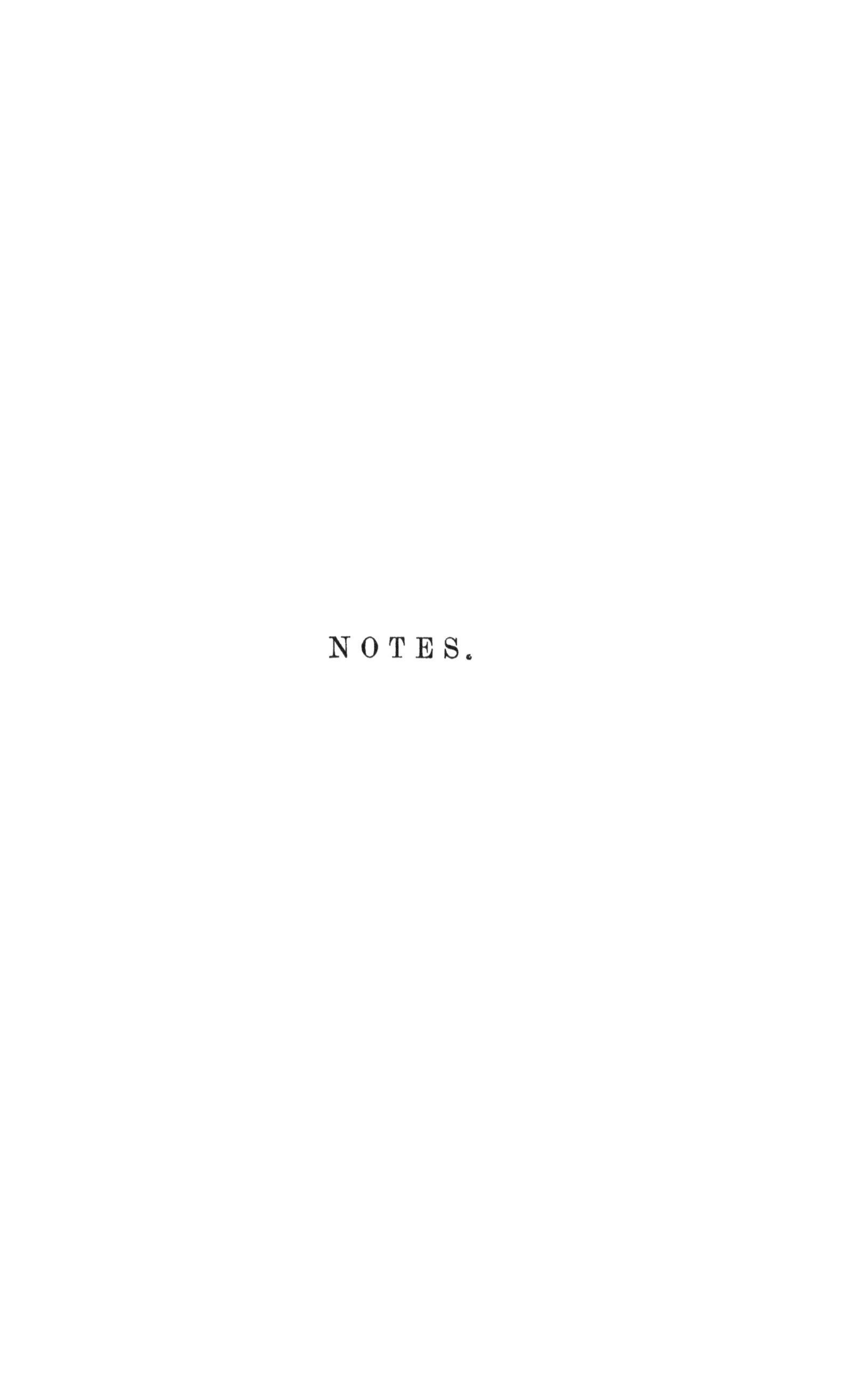

NOTES.

NOTES.

NOTE TO "THE BRIDE OF CORINTH."

The legend on which this poem is based is to be found in the treatise Περί θαυμασίων, by Phlegon of Tralles, a freedman of the Emperor Adrian, where it forms the first of the series of marvels recorded by that singular writer. The opening of the story is lost, but its nature is made sufficiently obvious by what remains.

"She passed," writes Phlegon, "to the door of the stranger's room, and there, by the shimmer of the lamp, beheld the damsel seated by the side of Machates. At this marvellous phenomenon she was unable to command herself; and, hastening to the damsel's mother, called with a loud voice to Charito and Demostratus to arise and go with her to their daughter; for that she had come back to life, and was even now closeted with the stranger in his room. Hearing this strange announcement, Charito, between fright at the intelligence and the bewilderment of the nurse, was at first distracted; then, remembering the daughter she had lost, she began to weep; and in the end, thinking the old woman crazed, she commanded her to betake herself to rest. To this the nurse rejoined by reproaches, insisting that she herself was in her right mind, but that the mother was unwilling from pure fear to behold her own daughter; and so at last Charito, partly constrained by the nurse, partly impelled by curiosity, repaired to the door of the stranger's apartment. But as a second message had been required to persuade her, a considerable space of time had, in the meanwhile, elapsed, so that by the time she reached the chamber they were both in bed. Looking in at the doorway, she thought she recognised the dress and features of her daughter; but being unable to satisfy herself of the truth, she conceived it best to make no disturbance. Moreover, she hoped, by rising in the morning betimes, to take the damsel by surprise; or, even if she should fail in this, then she thought to put Machates to question as to the matter, when of a surety, seeing how momentous it was, he would not speak that which was untrue. And so she withdrew noiselessly from the door. By daybreak, however, she found the damsel already gone, peradventure through chance, peradventure according to the will of some god. Disconcerted by her so sudden withdrawal, the mother narrated to her young guest all that she had seen, and, embracing his knees, besought him to tell her the truth, and to conceal nothing. Upon this the youth was at first smitten with consternation and sore confusion; at length, however, with difficulty he mentioned her name, Philinnion—recounted how she had come to him on the first occasion—with what fondness she had encountered him, and how she had said, that her visit was made without the knowledge of her parents. Furthermore, to confirm his tale, he opened a chest and showed a certain gift presented to him by the damsel; to wit, a golden ring, and also a scarf from her bosom, which she had left behind her on the previous night. On seeing these proofs, Charito shrieked, rent her robes in twain, tore the veil from her head, and, throwing herself upon the ground, kissed the well-known tokens, and broke forth anew into lamentations. When now the guest had reflected on what had transpired, and beheld them all weeping and wailing immoderately, as though they were now about for the first time to lay the damsel in the tomb, he began, all confounded though he was, to speak words of comfort to them, and vowed to give them intimation if she should return. Tranquillised by these assurances, Charito returned to her chamber, after conjuring the youth to deal truly with his promise. When night closed in, and the hour had come at which Philinnion was wont to visit him, the others held themselves in readiness for the tidings of her arrival. And truly come she did; and when she had entered at the accustomed time and seated herself upon the bed, Machates unconcernedly took his place beside her, longing nevertheless with all his heart to come at the bottom of the business; for he could not bring himself to think that it was a dead maiden with whom he had holden intercourse, seeing that she returned so punctually always at the same time, and ate and drank with him. Therefore did he mistrust the assurances of the nurse and of the parents, holding rather to the opinion that thieves had broken into and plundered the tomb, and sold the garments and the ornament of gold to the father of the damsel, who had in this wise made resort unto him. Wishing to be assured of the truth, therefore, he privily called his servants and sent them to the parents. Demostratus and Charito hastened with all speed to the apartment, and beholding the damsel there, they were for a time struck dumb with amazement at the wondrous apparition; but, recovering themselves, they ran forward with a great cry, and fell upon their daughter's neck. Then spoke Philinnion to them in this wise: 'Oh, mother and father, unjust and ungentle are ye, in that you grant me not to tarry unmolested with this stranger but for three days at my father's house. Now, therefore, because of your busy curiosity shall ye once again be made to mourn. But for me, I return unto my appointed place; for hither have I come not without the intervention of the gods.' When she had so spoken, she fell back dead once more, and lay there stretched out upon the bed."

The utmost excitement, says the chronicler, was occasioned in the household and the city by this singular event. The family-vault was searched, when all the bodies were found in their places, with the exception of Philinnion's, and, where that had lain, a steel ring belonging to the guest was discovered, and a parcel-gilt goblet, both of which she had received from her companion on the occasion of her first visit. By the advice of an augur of great reputation, the body was burnt outside the city walls—an expiatory sacrifice was made to Hermes and the Eumenides—lustrations were performed in the temples—sacrifices offered up for the Emperor and the public weal; and, as an appropriate consummation to the whole, the youth Machates laid violent hands upon himself.

It is interesting to observe how dexterously Goethe has availed him of the incidents narrated with so much circumstantiality in this striking legend; and what additional interest he has given it, by marking so distinctly the period when the old mythological faith was passing away under the influence of the Christian creed. With all reverence for the genius of Goethe, it is impossible to deny that he had strong Pagan tendencies, and these were never so forcibly exhibited as in the composition of this wonderful poem. It is said that it cost him only two days' labour, and, when completed, required no corrections; an effort which deserves to be recorded, for few poems in any language have been so complete and absolutely perfect in their structure as "The Bride of Corinth."

NOTE TO "THE ERL-KING."

Mr. Lewes, in his elaborate and deeply interesting Life of Goethe, has been at some pains to show that this ballad was neither a translation nor an adaptation from the Danish; and he has given a short account of the old Danish ballad, which was published in Herder's "Volkslieder," under the title of "Erl-Koenig's Tochter." Mr. Lewes is no doubt right in the main; but it seems to us very evident that Goethe took the hint from Herder's version, though he did not in this instance, as in "The Water-man," limit himself to the original. The term "Erl-King," which the Germans have adopted, seems to have puzzled many of our English writers. "Erle," in German, means alder-tree; and, misled by this derivation, modern mythologists have invented a spiritual guardian of the alders! In reality, "Erl" is a corrupted form of the word *Elve*, or *Elf*, common to the English and Danish languages. The old Norse ballad, which is to be found in the "Danske Viser," is entitled "Elveskud," or "The Elf-stroke," and the following is a very close translation of it, with the omission of the two last stanzas, and also of a *refrain*, which was commonly used by the professional reciters both of Denmark and Scotland.

THE ELF-STROKE.

Sir Oluf has ridden far and wide,
The folk to his wedding-feast to bid.

The elves they dance in the fairy ring,
And the Elf-King's daughter, she beckons to him.

"Now welcome, Sir Oluf, tarry a wee!
Step into the ring and dance with me."

"I must not dance, and I dare not stay,
To-morrow it is my wedding-day."

"Light down, Sir Oluf, and dance with me,
And two gold spurs I will give to thee:

"A sark, too, of silk, so white and fine,
My mother bleach'd it in pale moonshine."

"I must not dance, I dare not stay,
To-morrow it is my wedding-day."

"Light down, Sir Oluf, and dance with me,
And a heap of gold I'll give to thee."

"O well I like the golden glance,
But not for that with thee I'll dance."

"An' if thou wilt not dance with me,
A bane and a blight shall follow thee."

She struck him a blow right over the heart,
It chill'd him through with a wondrous smart.

Pale grew his cheek as he turn'd to ride;
"Now get thee home to thy winsome bride!"

And when to his castle door he sped,
Her mother stood waiting all a-dread.

"Now tell to me, Sir Oluf, my son,
What makes thy cheek so pale and wan?"

"O well may it be wan and pale,
I've seen the elf-folk in the vale!"

"Alas for thee, my son, my pride!
What shall I say to thy bonny bride?"

"Tell her that I'm to the forest bound,
To prove my horse and my good grey hound."

Right early, or ever the day had broke,
The bride she came with the bridal folk.

They dealt out meat, and they dealt out wine;
"Now where is Sir Oluf, this groom of mine?"

"Sir Oluf has gone to the forest bound,
To prove his steed and his good grey hound."

The bride she lifted the mantle red,
There lay Sir Oluf, and he was dead.

A.

www.ingramcontent.com/pod-product-compliance
Lightning Source LLC
LaVergne TN
LVHW010254110826
845151LV00004B/1470

* 9 7 8 1 4 2 5 5 2 2 5 8 2 *